PHIL COLLINS

THE PHIL COLLINS STORY

JOHNNY WALLER

ZOMBA BOOKS

Exclusively Distributed
In North America By

Cherry Lane Books

PORT CHESTER, NY 10573

First published in Great Britain in 1985 by Zomba Books,
Zomba House, 165–167 Willesden High Road, London NW10 2SG
and in the United States of America by

© Johnny Waller

ISBN 0 946391 78 5

Typeset by Cambridge Photosetting Services, Cambridge
Printed by Thetford Press Limited, Thetford, Norfolk
Designed by Tina Dutton
Cover designed by Steve O'Leary
Production services by Book Production Consultants, Cambridge

First Edition

CONTENTS

The author would like to thank the following people for their invaluable help in researching and writing this book. First and foremost, heartfelt thanks to Marianne for undying patience and encouragement.

But also, thanks to Solly and Robin for covering up for my absences.

Thanks to all at the Virgin Records Press Office – Ellie, Mark, Sian, Nicole and Lorraine.

Thanks to Lee-Ellen Newman at Charisma Records.

Thanks to everyone at Zomba for constant guidance – Dede, Louise, Lyndsay and especially John Tobler.

Thanks for endless advice, inspiration and factual co-operation to Hugh Fielder, friend to the stars!

Thanks to June Collins, Phil's mum, for being friendly and helpful.

And finally, thanks to my mum and dad for starting the whole thing!

Author's note: This biography is intended as an examination of the career of Phil Collins as an artist – those readers who require more details about Genesis are recommended to read the following books, which I have liberally consulted for my own research:

'The Book Of Genesis' by Hugh Fielder
'Turn It On Again' by Geoff Parkyn
'From One Fan To Another' by Armando Gallo.

In many ways, JOHNNY WALLER is the ideal journalist to write a detailed, sympathetic biography of Phil Collins, simply because of their remarkably similar backgrounds.

Both were born in Chiswick, West London, and showed an impressive talent for soccer before turning to careers in the entertainment world. Both are short, blond and stocky. And both survived devastating divorces which directly affected their artistic output.

Johnny Waller is now 30 and lives in Brixton with his girlfriend Marianne. He has interviewed pop singers, footballers, comedians, actresses, poets and boxers and yet still believes in the power of the spoken word. His favourite author is William Shakespeare. He also enjoys watching 'Coronation Street', playing squash and eating vast amounts of Marianne's famous lasagne – though preferably not at the same time!

Mr Waller has previously co-authored (with his friend and colleague Steve Rapport) the definitive Eurythmics biography 'Sweet Dreams' and is currently studying to become the jam donut champion of the Tony Hancock Fan Club (Outer Hebrides Branch). No flowers, please, by request.

WHO IS THIS MAN?

Speeding through the sky, smashing through the sound barrier, is a superstar of the eighties.

He's short, stocky and balding . . . the most unlikely looking star since Elton John: obviously not a film actor! His sense of humour is legend, but he's not known as a comic – he's a singing hero to millions: the only modern rock star who commands the vast loyalty and popularity necessary to enable him play at both of the two huge Live Aid benefit concerts – one in London, the other in Philadelphia – on the same day!

He's had Number One hit singles and albums, performed sell-out tours world-wide and is in constant demand as a producer noted for his work with Philip Bailey, Eric Clapton, Adam Ant and Frida from Abba, as well as being one of the best rock drummers in the world. As if that wasn't enough, apart from his phenomenally successful solo career, he's also the singer and drummer for an internationally adored rock band called Genesis.

So who is this man and what drives him on?
Turn the page and begin to discover the truth about . . .

PHIL COLLINS!

1

GROWING UP. . .

Philip David Charles Collins was born in Chiswick, West London on 30th January 1951, which makes his astrological sign Aquarius.

He was educated at Chiswick County Grammar School, where he briefly indulged ambitions of becoming a professional soccer player! In fact, he showed enough potential to be picked to play for the Chiswick Grammar School team, but tended to be too nervous during big games and his dreams of World Cup glory soon faded.

But by now his mind was already focussed on something much more dramatic – pop music!

"When I was five, I was given a toy drum but my parents would hide it in the basement. It was a tin drum – so noisy – but I was really into it, so my uncles Reg and Len made me a drum kit. It was built up on a criss-cross base with triangles, tambourines, cymbals and little toy drums attached by poles. It all fitted into a suitcase.

"I remember sitting in the front room playing along to the television, and I have very vivid memories of playing along to 'Sunday Night At The London Palladium'."

And so Phil would bash away for hours while the family were trying to watch TV!

Luckily, though, his parents were not only tolerant of such boisterous hobbies – they actively encouraged him! And so he soon made his first public appearance, playing drums in the Converted Cruiser Club (now the Richmond Yacht Club) at the age of five.

But Phil also showed a talent for dramatic roles.

"The first one was Buttons in 'Cinderella' – and I've got photographic evidence of that! I was also Humpty Dumpty in panto there," he admits sheepishly.

"You see, my mum and dad had this boat – only a small one, not a yacht or anything – on the Thames at Richmond and we were members of the Richmond Yacht Club on Eel Pie Island. Being the youngest cadet, I was always getting called upon for the club entertainments.

"The whole family got involved in it – brother, sister, mum, dad – so no-one bothered about being thought a twerp."

But by now Phil was also serious about playing music.

"There was this guy across the street who had a real set of drums, so I exchanged my train set with him for them.

"The first records I played along with were 'It Only Took A Minute' by Joe Brown and 'Dance On' by the Shadows" – both Top Ten records in 1962. Eventually – on his twelfth birthday – his parents had bought him a full-size kit.

Phil was also a keen fan and remembers that the first record he ever bought was either the *Please Please Me* LP by the Beatles or the first Rolling Stones LP.

The Collins family had always been artistically inclined – especially on Phil's father side – with the emphasis on making their own entertainment. His dad, Greville, was a fine singer, while Phil's older brother Clive – now a noted cartoonist – and sister, Carole, a keen ice-skater, did a double act. His mother, June, by contrast, discovered that her talents were behind the scenes where she worked as a theatrical agent, running the Barbara Speake Stage Agency.

As a kid, Philip was blessed with a cherubic face and impish grin topped off with a mass of golden hair, and his mum soon realised that he had exactly the right natural cuteness for the world of child modelling and she arranged for him to appear on the covers of various knitting catalogues.

Unfortunately, this irresistible charm didn't help him when he first fell in love.

"There was a girl at school called Lynda, I was eleven and it was real love. But Lynda wasn't in love with me."

However, he was more than just another pretty face with a broken heart and he soon proved this by displaying a remarkable talent for acting, which resulted in June Collins booking him for small parts in radio and TV shows, and sending him to auditions for occasional film roles.

Finally Phil achieved what he thought was to be his big break – a small (non-speaking) part alongside the Beatles in their first film, 'A Hard Day's Night'.

"You can't *see* me in 'Hard Day's Night'," he laughs. "I just happen to like the fact that I was in a Beatles film."

His mother explains that "It was a non-event really! Phil was just one of a hundred kids we supplied for one scene. Because I was the agent, whenever I got a call like that, I would send him along."

When Phil was fourteen, his mother received a much more potentially important call – one asking for a juvenile actor to star at the New Theatre in London's West End for a new production of 'Oliver' (a musical by Lionel Bart based on Charles Dickens' classic novel 'Oliver Twist'). And he got the part!

"I played the part of The Artful Dodger – it was probably the most enjoyable acting experience I've ever had. I mean, it didn't require much acting – it was my personality anyway, but my dad was very proud of the fact that I was in the West End as an actor. I got fifteen pounds a week – not bad for a teenager!"

And Phil also had to sing – each night crooning the pickpockets' anthem 'You've Got To Pick A Pocket Or Two'.

These were great times for young Phil – and he recounts that the funniest experience he had was trying to do a grand entrance as The Artful Dodger when the revolving stage had broken and was being pushed around.

And his worst experience? "Trying to sing in the same show when my voice was breaking."

This glorious run – his first taste of the big-time and audience adulation – lasted nine months until his voice broke, at which time he formally left the Grammar School and started attending classes at Barbara Speake Stage School.

But he was hardly back behind his desk before he returned to the small screen, appearing in a succession of BBC television plays and doing voice-overs for 'Junior Points Of View' before he returned briefly to 'Oliver', this time taking the adult role of Noah Claypole.

"Because I went to drama school, I didn't have much formal schooling as there was never much time for lessons. I've always tried to work out what is right and then follow it. I believe in the old adage 'do as you would be done by'."

His acting career continued in fits and starts – he appeared on TV in Stubby Kaye's 'Silver Star Show' in 1966 and was an extra in Walt Disney's 1967 spectacular 'Chitty Chitty Bang Bang' – but gradually Phil became less interested in acting and yearned for a career in music.

Occasionally he would attend auditions not knowing what they were for, only to discover that they were for dancing – "which I hated. I passed one, it was for a promotional tour for Smiths Crisps which did the rounds of all the Locarnos and Mecca places.

"There were four of us – two blokes and two girls. We'd go out on the dance floor and this place would be packed with skinheads. I had this completely white outfit – white t-shirt, white trousers, white patent boots – and I had to go out and dance in front of these skinheads.

"Of course, we got heckled and stuff, especially when we had to demonstrate the dance to encourage people on to the floor. It was horrible. God I hated it!"

More and more Phil turned to music, preferring to stay at home alone with his drum kit rather than attend auditions for acting roles he didn't really want.

"I used to get phone calls offering him parts," recalls his mum June. "But he used to say, 'No, mum – you *know* what I want to do . . .'."

The last acting that Phil did was in a dreadful children's film for Saturday morning cinema called 'Calamity The Cow'!

"I played the eldest of four kids in a family. The idea was

that we had a cow which was going to win the county show. Anyway, the cow got stolen and we found it just in time to enter the competition.

"I was sixteen at the time and I fell out with the director. When you're sixteen, you don't want to look a berk, you have your own ideas. I had ideas about the way I wanted to play the part and how I should deliver certain lines, but he wanted me to act as if I were about eleven or twelve. We used to have lots of arguments, so he wrote me out of the film when I was away on holiday!

"I thought 'If this is what goes on . . . I want to drum!' "

2

PHIL'S FLAMING YOUTH

Once he gave up acting, Phil threw himself whole-heartedly into drumming.

"My first group was The Real Thing. We all took it very seriously and used to rehearse every day after school. I used to sing and drum at the same time, because no-one else could sing. Andy (Andrea), who later became my wife, used to be one of the back-up singers.

"We used to model ourselves on the Who and The Action and do a lot of Motown stuff. It was a good group."

Good group or not, The Real Thing failed to make much of an impression with the general public and soon split up. Phil drifted from band to band — most of them now all forgotten except the actual names . . . The Charge, Zox And The Radar Boys, The Cliff Charles Blues Band and Freehold.

He recalls the strangest gig ever: "One with an early band, Freehold. We played a boy's equivalent of a convent school in Oxford — there was a room full of Friar Tucks."

Next came the Gladiators: "Basically a four-piece soul group and they wanted musicians to back them. Hickory was the band that was formed to back them and I was brought in on drums. Then we started getting better than the Gladiators, so we split from them and changed our name to Flaming Youth."

Apart from Phil on drums and percussion, the other Youths were Gordon Smith on guitar and bass, Ronnie Caryl on bass and twelve-string guitar and Brian Chatton on organ and piano. All four of them shared vocal duties.

The band were at that time managed by Ken Howard and Alan Blaikely who were also noted songwriters, having achieved chart success with The Herd and The Tremeloes.

They had written a batch of eight songs conforming to a storyline about the last spaceship leaving a burning planet Earth, basing the plot structure around Holst's 'Planet Suite' and using the hymn 'Immortal Invisible' as the basis for one of the songs, 'From Now On'.

Howard and Blaikely then put up the finance for some time at London's famous De Lane Lea studio and told the band they had two weeks to record a complete album.

The final product, by now called *Ark II*, was released by Fontana in November 1969, while Phil was just eighteen and was seized on immediately by a music press looking for new talent.

Melody Maker granted it the accolade of 'Pop Album Of The Month' (above new releases by such artists as Mott The Hoople, Creedence Clearwater Revival, The Small Faces and Alice Cooper!) and called it "a magnificent first album".

The rave review referred to "adult music beautifully played with nice, tight harmonies", describing the lyrics (all written by Howard and Blaikely) as "biting, very clever, sometimes savage and extremely witty."

For some strange reason, the LP sleeve showed the eight songs as being credited to the group themselves! Phil was supposed to have co-written three of them and be the sole composer of one track, the appallingly-titled 'Space Child'. Most likely, this confusion was caused either by the group's own determination to be regarded as song-writers (even if they weren't!) or as a method of claiming extra income by means of publishing royalties.

"We had a burst of publicity when our album came out," recalls Phil. "That was about it – a blaze of publicity and very little work."

At the time of the album's release, on Friday 14th September 1969, Flaming Youth played a major London concert at the Lyceum in the Strand. It was advertised in the music press as "The First Public Performance of *Ark II* by Flaming Youth, with full orchestra and choir and the Ray McVay Brass". It was an ambitious – and not entirely successful – venture for an admission of a pound or sixteen shillings in advance.

"It was very schizophrenic because we used to go to gigs and play our regular band stuff at the beginning of the set and then follow that with the album material. Mainly we used to take other people's numbers apart and put them back together again so you could hardly recognise them! People who'd liked the first part of the show generally hated the second."

Fontana didn't seem to have much faith in either the group or the record – although they did release one track, 'Guide Me Orion', as a single – and Phil soon became disenchanted with the whole situation.

"After a year," says Phil, "I decided that it was going nowhere and I left. I auditioned for various bands – Vinegar Joe, which had Robert Palmer, and Manfred Mann's Earth Band or Chapter Three I think it was called then.

"I was never successful at the auditions, funnily enough. I thought I was pretty good, but there was always someone better than me."

3

GENESIS: THE EARLY YEARS

But Phil Collins still hadn't given up hope of becoming a drummer with a top band. Suddenly he was given the chance to make his dreams come true: he received an invitation to audition for a new group called Genesis.

They were a bunch of public school pretentious eccentrics whose music was by turns enchanting, pompous, epic, and dramatically over-ambitious. It was, in short, what the British music press called 'progressive rock' and what American critics referred to as 'art-rock'.

But it was also melodic and addictive to a hard core of fans who had become captivated by the band's brand of twisting, undulating tales.

Genesis had originally formed at Charterhouse, a prestigious public school in Surrey. Peter Gabriel and Tony Banks entered Charterhouse in September 1963 as thirteen year-olds. Both of them were shy nervous boys and hated the place immediately – Peter later referred to it as "this cold, merciless environment" – but swiftly became firm friends due to a shared passion for The Beatles, who had just taken the pop world by storm.

They had much more in common: both came from musical families who had forced piano lessons on the unwilling children and both had rebelled by refusing to co-operate. However, Tony was then fuelled by the enthusiasm of a Charterhouse master and started playing once more. He was soon attempting to copy the rough arrangements he heard in the pop songs on the radio and the soul records he and Peter adored, especially those by Otis Redding and James Brown.

For Peter, the piano was a lost cause. His favourite instrument was the human voice and he'd sing along to the entire soul catalogue of Stax Records given the chance.

"I remember the billiard room vividly; it was the only place we could play music. It had this really beaten up, old Dansette record player in a wooden cabinet. You could only play it for an hour and half every day.

"I used to take my Otis Redding records in there and turn them up full volume and dance until I was in a frenzied sweat. This ritual gave me an immense feeling of relief."

Peter was spellbound by the wild rhythms in such records and he decided to emulate them by becoming a drummer, first in a dance band called M'Lords and then in a soul group called The Spoken Word.

"I wanted to be a drummer at that point, but at the same time, I realised that I also wanted to write songs. The first song I wrote was called 'Sammy The Slug'. I don't think it was particularly memorable!"

It seemed almost inevitable that Peter and Tony should collaborate on songs and then form their own group, called The Garden Wall, which also featured a trumpeter and drummer. They subsequently became aware of another Charterhouse band, The Anon, which had been formed by Anthony "Ant" Phillips and Mike Rutherford.

"We were just doing Stones numbers," recalls Ant. "These really caught the imagination of the school and we did some beat concerts. We played for about a year and a half having a great time.

"I used to listen to Tony playing Beatles songs on the piano," recalls Ant, "and I would strum along with the guitar. That's how we really began. Gradually I became aware of this strange individual who would occasionally stand on the dining-room table and sing – this was Peter."

In July 1966 The Garden Wall played an end-of-term school concert supporting The Anon – and afterwards, both groups split up!

From these ashes came a nascent phoenix. They recorded a demo tape in a friend's studio. "Basically it was Mike and Ant recording their songs" explains Tony. "Chris Stewart was on drums and I was asked along to play keyboards. Peter arrived on the second day and we persuaded Ant – who had been doing the vocals – that Peter had a better voice."

And so Gabriel sang five Rutherford–Phillips compositions plus one song that he and Tony Banks had written, 'She's Beautiful'. "And of course, their song was far better than any of ours!" admits Ant.

The resultant demo tape was sent to Jonathan King, an ex-pupil of Charterhouse and fast-rising pop entrepreneur and self-promoted star. He'd already scored a Top Five hit single with the cute 'Everyone's Gone To The Moon' (back in 1965 when he was only twenty-one) and was now working at Decca Records.

Prompted to listen to the tape because of the Charterhouse connection, King found himself actually liking it and even thinking "there are some interesting song ideas here".

He promptly christened the still-unnamed group Genesis ("His first suggestion was Gabriel's Angels which appealed to me!" laughs Peter. "Though somehow this didn't seem to register with the others.") and signed them to a five-year publishing deal for the princely sum of forty pounds. Luckily, with invaluable parental guidance, the group managed to have the deal renegotiated to a one-year deal with a one-year option.

"We were excited just by the fact that anyone was interested in our songs," recalls Tony Banks. "We would have signed for life at that stage."

King's ear for obvious pop commerciality had detected strong possibilities in the Genesis song structures – despite their tendency to be far too elaborate in their arrangements – and he encouraged them to write some more simple verse-chorus-verse tunes with catchy hooks.

Two further recording sessions failed to produce what King was looking for – he complained the group were producing songs that were "too complex" – so Peter and Tony responded by writing a Bee Gees pastiche, 'The

Silent Sun', which King ironically thought was a sure-fire hit.

The single picked up a great review from Chris Welch in Melody Maker and was even played by Kenny Everett on Radio One! Mike: "We thought 'here we go!' – we even went out and bought our gear for Top Of The Pops."

After the commercial failure of another single – 'A Winter's Tale' – King suggested that they should record an album, which the band regarded as their natural medium anyway.

From Genesis To Revelation was produced by King and recorded in just one day, featuring drummer John Silver. It was released in March 1969 and virtually nobody liked it – not even the group themselves.

"It was supposed to be the history of the universe," explained Peter. "Altogether a very duff concept. I think there are some things that showed we had melody-writing potential but that's about all I can say."

Another single – comprising two tracks taken from the LP, 'Where The Sour Turns To Sweet' and 'In Hiding' – was released to universal disdain and King began to lose interest in the whole project.

"He was the kind of guy who got very excited about something and then he would go off and do something else," rationalises Mike now. "Finally we lied and said we'd split up. He let us go and we reformed a month later."

But for the first half of 1969, Genesis were an aimless outfit with no outlet for their music. Banks had gone on to Sussex University, Gabriel was considering The London School of Film Technique and drummer John Silver had gone off to university in America – the very future of the group was in doubt, even though both Phillips and Rutherford were enthusiastic to become professional musicians. In August they recorded a new demo tape at Regent Sound Studios.

Tony Banks: "We took this tape round and the reaction we got from it was pretty bad. Everyone said it was terrible."

Ironically this negative reaction spurred on the four of

them to make a real go of it, so they recruited new drummer John Mayhew and locked themselves away in a country cottage for intensive rehearsals. When they emerged with a fully-structured set which climaxed each evening with the new-found aggression of 'The Knife', they soon built up a loyal following on the thriving club circuit.

This culminated in a residency upstairs at Ronnie Scott's Club and inspired passing interest from a couple of record companies – Island and the Moody Blues' own label, Threshold.

However, before either of those labels could make up their minds, Genesis were approached by John Anthony, an A & R scout from the newly-formed Charisma record company. He had seen the first performance at Ronnie Scott's and had been so impressed that he returned the following week, this time bringing with him his managing director Tony Stratton-Smith, a former sports journalist who had launched his own label to nurture home-grown talent.

Stratton-Smith was equally convinced of the band's talent – "They were so incredibly good," – and signed them immediately. He has since described them as: "Rather like a young classic racehorse – if you work them too hard too early they'll just burn out."

But Stratton-Smith had faith in their music and regarded the group as a major talent for the long term. "I saw them as a band that was still putting together its own language – an album band and a band to whom you had to make a two or three year commitment, whatever the cost."

In the first year, the cost was minimal as each member of the band was paid a retainer of just ten pounds a week, but the cosy atmosphere at the new label – whose other artists included Lindisfarne, The Nice and Van Der Graaf Generator – suited Genesis and gave them confidence in their future.

Unfortunately, their first record for Charisma – the *Trespass* album – lacked both focus and direction, ironically relying far too much on other contemporary influences such as King Crimson.

The distinctive mellotron sound was very much in vogue at that time, but Genesis were much less successful in recording the guitar tracks.

"We still had no idea of recording techiques," admitted Tony Banks afterwards, "and for 'Stagnation' Mike and Ant recorded the guitar parts three or four different times, the original idea being to choose between them. In the end we mixed all the guitar parts onto one track, which meant we got a very blurry sound – it wasn't what we intended at all."

But at least Genesis were making great strides as songwriters outside of the restrictive channel of trite three-minute pop tunes – 'The Knife', for instance, had been inspired by a book about the life of Ghandi!

"Ant and I used to enjoy playing with words," explained Pete. "We would write poems that had nothing to do with songs. He was more into flowery, romantic visions, whereas I was into the darker and altogether more mysterious side of life. When I look back, it really makes me cringe – but I guess it was all part of growing up."

After the *Trespass* album was released in October 1970, Anthony Phillips amazed the rest of the band by announcing he was quitting.

He later explained his decision: "This has often been presented as 'musical differences' and, although there was some truth in this, the main reason was that I started getting incredible stage fright. That's the truth. I was mentally and physically debilitated."

In addition, he became frustrated and dissatisfied with the whole sound of the band – "It all sounded so wrong that I used to come off stage feeling terrible."

Ant's departure was a dreadful blow for the whole band, both musically – his guitar work and song-writing had become an integral part of the band's character – and personally, especially for Tony, who had felt really close to him. "We'd all been together since school and it always seemed that there was a certain magic. It was an incredible blow – for a while I thought about giving up too."

Instead, Genesis agreed to have a major re-assessment. Obviously they needed a new guitarist, but equally important was finding the right overall balance musically.

Consequently, drummer John Mayhew was asked to leave: according to Mike Rutherford, "I don't think John was that surprised, actually. Although he worked so hard and so well, he was a slow learner and didn't produce many ideas."

Mayhew was the third drummer to depart in as many years. The band were beginning to despair of ever finding the right person, but were determined to make strenuous efforts in one final attempt.

Finally they agreed to run an advert in the classified pages of Melody Maker: "Tony Stratton-Smith requires drummer sensitive to acoustic music, and acoustic twelve-string guitarist."

4

FROM GENESIS TO. . .

In September 1970, Phil Collins found himself at a loose end and so started looking for a new group to drum with.

"At the time, I was a huge fan of certain groups and I used to go and see Yes every week at the Marquee. I happened to be next to a bloke in the audience who told me that they were looking for a new drummer as Bill Bruford was leaving to go to university.

"So I went backstage and introduced myself to their singer, Jon Anderson. He said 'Well, great man, great. Give us a ring on Tuesday and come down for an audition.'

"I never rang. I never went.

"I've always wondered about that, because I knew the songs backwards. I'm sure I would have got the job and would have ended up in Yes."

Also in the audience at the Marquee that night was Tony Stratton-Smith, whom Phil pestered to reveal the name of the group from his advert. Eventually Tony told him it was Genesis.

"I'd noticed their name a lot in the back of Melody Maker," recalls Phil. "They seemed to play a lot of gigs. I thought I was onto something and that Strat might even give me the job because I knew him. But I still had to do the audition."

So Collins turned up at Peter Gabriel's parents' house ready to show what he could do and was greeted by Mike — wearing only dressing-gown and slippers — who suggested that while the band tried out a couple of other drummers first, Phil should have a swim in the private swimming pool!

Of course, such casual elegance was taken for granted by Genesis who had all been to public school at Charterhouse, while Collins was a working-class kid who had been brought up in the West London district of Hounslow!

"I just couldn't believe it," he says. "I thought 'God, this is incredible!' There was certainly a class difference between us.

"But I was precocious and self-confident and I think that gave me a good rapport with them."

Phil's confidence – not to mention his talent – impressed the group the moment he sat at the drum-stool.

"We auditioned about fifteen drummers," remembers Tony. "Phil was about third and Peter and I immediately thought he was the best. He played everything we gave him really perfectly."

Phil had come to the audition well-prepared for whatever the band might demand, and was also helped by watching the first couple of hopefuls trying their best.

"I knew all the parts they were auditioning on; they were asking everybody to play bits of 'The Knife' and bits of 'Stagnation' – a mixture of gentle and heavy stuff. I knew it backwards by the time it came round to my turn.

"Not only did I know it backwards, but I was pretty quick, having got used to playing different types of music in various different bands. I think I must have made it look very easy."

The decision was never in doubt and Phil was quickly confirmed as the band's new drummer, although before he played his first gig with the band, he spent two weeks decorating houses for a friend – "The only time I've done a proper day's work in my life!"

"It didn't take me long to realise that Genesis was a very special thing. I'd been used to playing with tacky groups . . . but this did have a quality about it that was something different."

Suddenly the band adopted a more professional attitude. "There was a definite change when Phil came into the band," agreed Peter Gabriel. "He was a real drummer – something that I was never convinced of with Chris Stewart or John Mayhew.

"Up until then, we were just a group of fairly ramshackle musicians, trying hard to communicate through our music. Most of our ideas were in the form of songs and riffs and melodies – playing our instruments was somewhat secondary.

"Phil was not really a writer at that point, but a musician: and a very good and professional one. He changed our attitudes and brought us closer together as a band."

However, the other members still felt constrained by their quintessentially reserved English upbringing, which readily confused the more open, affable Collins.

"I was used to bands that were 'all mates' and if you wanted to say something, you came out and said it, or hit somebody or whatever."

Genesis were very different. "There were incredible arguments after I joined," Phil said. "I didn't understand all the internal frictions, I didn't really know what the hell was going on. It seemed like a very tense situation."

Matters improved as soon as they started playing gigs. Not having yet found a new guitarist to replace Ant, they played a string of concerts as a quartet.

"It was quite frightening at times playing as a four piece" is Tony Bank's recollection. "It was probably then that I advanced most as a musician as I was required to play two parts together on stage. By the end of that period, we were starting to come together."

They were all agreed that they really still needed a full-time guitarist and so they recruited Mick Barnard from an Aylesbury group called Farm for a couple of gigs to see how it would go. It didn't quite work out, mainly because Genesis had progressed considerably since Phil had joined and – by comparision – Mick was fairly inexperienced and didn't really fit in.

Eventually they resorted to a tried and trusted method of finding replacements: the Melody Maker classified section! This time, though, Peter decided to *answer* an advert

– "Guitarist/writer seeks receptive musicians determined to strive beyond existing stagnant musical forms."

The guitarist-writer-advertiser was invited down to see the band play a free Christmas concert at London's Lyceum and he was sufficiently impressed to join soon afterwards. His name was Steve Hackett and he'd previously been in a group called Quiet World.

With their line-up now confirmed as a solid five-piece, Genesis began 1971 by touring (bottom of the bill, naturally!) with label-mates Van Der Graaf Generator and Lindisfarne: this was notable mostly for Peter jumping offstage into a seething audience at Aylesbury – and breaking his ankle!

While they waited for the break to heal, the band began rehearsing material for their next album at Tony Stratton-Smith's house in Sussex, and then recorded the songs at Trident Studio in London with producer John Anthony. The third Genesis LP, *Nursery Cryme*, was duly released in November.

Looking back now, the band have mixed feelings about it. "*Nursery Cryme* is not one of my favourite albums," admits Phil openly. "It sounds as if everybody's playing with two hands on the keyboard. There's huge chords, as well as two guitars and a really big drum sound. Pete's voice is very thick, and as a result, it sounds as if it is all being squeezed onto this bit of tape."

However, it was worthy of mention for the track 'For Absent Friends' which featured the lead vocals of Phil Collins!

Tony Banks: "It dawned on me that *Nursery Cryme* really was no improvement on *Trespass* and I accepted it as one of those things." This was pretty much the same attitude adopted by the record-buying public, except for Italy where the album reached the Top Five!

Today Italy, tomorrow er, . . . Belgium!

"I think it was at Pete's wedding" laughs Tony, "that we first heard that *Trespass* had got to Number One in Belgium – whatever that meant – and we were amazed. We had only done one little gig in Belgium, a little club where we had set up in phalanx form."

While Britain (apart from Aylesbury!) and America continued to ignore the band, Europe began to welcome Genesis with increasing fervour.

Phil: "Belgium and Italy were the two main places that liked us. It was really all down to Belgium festivals. I remember throwing up on the boat on the way over there and limping home exhausted."

By the time they played a seven-date tour of Italy in April 1972 such was their success on the continent that *Nursery Cryme* had risen to Number Four in the Italian album charts – three places below their great friends and rivals Van Der Graaf Generator who were Number One with *Pawn Hearts.*

British audiences were still only luke-warm about the band's music but the crowd in Lincoln at the Great Western Express festival were stunned when Genesis walked on stage and Peter Gabriel revealed that he had shaved the top of his head! The large crowd were unresponsive to the music – possibly it wasn't best suited to an outdoor festival – but this was just the start of Peter's cavalier foray into the world of theatrical presentation.

"As the front-man, I was very conscious of how we were going down with our audiences," he explained. "Phil was the critical element in terms of the music, and I was the critical element in terms of style."

One day, Paul Conroy at Charisma suggested they involve themselves in more visual trickery by getting someone to dress up in a red dress and fox's head to promote their forthcoming LP, to be called *Foxtrot.*

"I think he really fancied doing it himself" reckoned Peter. "And I thought, 'Well, damn it, if we're going to do it, I want to do it. I want to be the centre of attention!'"

And so it came to pass, at a boxing ring in Dublin.

"I remember being very nervous as I walked onto the stage in the middle of a number. The audience was shocked by seeing the weirdness of a man dressed up in woman's clothing and a fox mask – but I loved it!

"I always really felt that the others only tolerated this new visual direction. They knew they were benefitting from it, but they weren't totally happy about it. Maybe it was just because they felt I was steering our music in a way they didn't want it to be steered."

But Phil and the others were actually impressed by Peter – both for his warped inventiveness and his bravery. "We were amused that he had the gall to go out and do it.

"But our songs and words often had more to them than met the eye – they weren't regular rock'n'roll lyrics. So when Peter started coming in wearing these masks, it was just an extension of the fantasy element."

When Genesis returned to London to headline at the Rainbow – at that time the most prestigious venue on the UK rock circuit – Melody Maker ran a front cover depicting Pete in the fox's head outfit. Immediately the band's infamy soared, and with it their pulling power. Overnight they doubled their fee from £300 to £600.

"Suddenly people had something to write about," reasoned Phil. "You can't really write about crashing cymbals, thudding drums and the swirling keyboards for very long. They needed some new angle – and suddenly Peter had given it to them. The Rainbow concert was definitely the beginning of all that."

When *Foxtrot* was released by Charisma in October, it received rave reviews in both Melody Maker and Sounds. It also charted in Britain (it peaked at Number Twelve), which left the obvious next target as . . . America!

And so, in December 1972, Tony Stratton-Smith sent Genesis over to New York for a short pioneering US tour.

"Tour's too grand a word for it actually" cautions Phil. "We did two gigs. The first was at the University in Boston, and we arrived there thinking 'OK, America – are you ready for us?' and I'd be surprised if there were even thirty people in the audience."

In many ways, the next night – an important charity concert at the Philharmonic Hall in New York – was even worse. "The whole gig was a complete nightmare" says Tony Banks. "It was full of mistakes," adds Steve Hackett. "We were very nervous and terribly tired, physically and mentally, and my amp packed up just before we were going to go on."

More than that, after the set Mike came straight off stage,

stormed back to the dressing-room and threw his bass in the corner. He was convinced the whole show had been a disaster.

Phil, by total contrast thought it was great – "the audience loved it.

"I felt it had gone all right, but Tony and Mike have always been more affected by setbacks: they want every gig to be perfect. We had a few drinks and everyone cooled down a bit. I think we all thought America had taken to us. That was it, we've played New York, so now we're big in America. But twenty miles down the road they hadn't even heard of us."

Nevertheless, this gig formed the groundwork for future Genesis tours of America, allowing the band to return in March of the following year for a month-long visit of East coast cities.

On their return to London, Genesis began planning for their first major tour of Britain, which climaxed at the Rainbow again. A review by Chris Welch in Melody Maker said: "It was one of those great turning-point concerts when a group receives the accolade of semi-hysteria from loyalist fans come to celebrate a triumph. And undoubtedly the band responded by giving one of the best performances of their career."

For the individual members of Genesis this should have been the highlight of their career so far, but there was a degree of internal friction looming that threatened to take the shine off their glory.

Peter Gabriel had begun to exaggerate his visual expressions – "When things were getting too twee and pretty and English public school, I would try and introduce a little weirdness or menace so that there was a darker side."

This often took the shape of outlandish or ghoulish costumes which unsettled the rest of the group and confused or even intimidated audiences. At a gig in Toronto, Peter had been heckled then physically attacked by disgruntled fans.

Meanwhile, the rest of the band looked ordinary almost to the point of anonymity as the spotlight (literally) centred on Gabriel. "The visual thing started working for us in a way," explains Phil. "Pete became the obvious focus of attention. But eventually that started back-firing internally.

"I know I felt frustrated – we would play a good set or a bad set and people would just ignore it and say 'Yeah, you looked good tonight'."

Such problems and complaints were temporarily shelved as the band came off the road – they'd been touring solidly for almost two years – in order to write some new material. Despite the group's natural reservations, Charisma used this break to release a live album imaginatively entitled *Genesis Live*.

It was largely Stratton-Smith's idea, as he willingly accepts. "I finally convinced them to go for the idea because it came out at a very low price. It was an attempt to broaden the audience and in that sense I think it worked."

Actually the band were surprised at the quality of the album itself – "We never felt that we sounded as good live as we did on record," says Phil. "In fact, it was the reverse – we always sounded more gutsy on stage than we did on record."

With the live LP nestling in the album charts, Genesis prepared for the next studio venture.

Phil: "We rehearsed at the same two places as we had done for *Foxtrot* – Una Billings' School Of Dancing in Shepherd's Bush and at this doctor's house in Chessington. The doctor had six daughters and lots of dachshunds and between them the daughters and the dachshunds drove us mad.

"We seemed to be spreading ourselves all over the place and it wasn't really coming together that well."

The main problem was simply time – they had too much of it! Given three months to come up with an album's worth of new material, they lacked the essential pressure that gets the adrenalin flowing.

Tony Banks summed it up as "A period when nothing seemed to happen. We just went over the same bits again. I began to think 'Is this really worth it?'.

"We got very frustrated and I seem to remember Phil in particular went through a very bad time during this period."

For Collins, the one bright spot was 'More Fool Me', a song which he both sang and co-wrote. For the first time, it allowed him to escape from behind his drum-kit during live shows and even become the centre of attention, if only for one song!

But overall, the new material suffered from a lack of economy; perhaps the main problem was that they were simply trying too hard.

"I think we were getting conscious of technique on this album," explains Mike. "The fact that we'd become competent players gave us confidence to play fast phrases and to be clever. There are some moments when we're all trying to be too clever!

"But at the same time, you've got to try for something, to move on to the next stage."

For Genesis, the next stage was a hit single! The new album, *Selling England By The Pound* was released in October 1973 and six months later, it was decided to release an LP track as a single. To everyone's surprise, 'I Know What I Like (In Your Wardrobe)' reached Number Twenty-one.

Suddenly external success magnified the internal disagreements. For a band like Genesis – not content merely to recreate fifties rock'n'roll and sixties beat – democracy and the fragile artistic ego sat together uneasily.

"We always used to have strong territorial rights about who played what," reveals Phil. "I remember recording 'I Know What I Like' and, while Tony was away one afternoon, Peter had an idea and switched Tony's gear on and played and recorded it.

"Tony came in the next day, we played him the track and he said 'What's that?'. Pete said 'That's a mellotron thing I did last night.' And Tony said 'I'm the keyboard player'. Pete started to argue and sparks flew. Someone else probably walked out. The usual story."

Pete agreed: "If we had been mature enough to avoid these petty problems, the band would have worked a lot better."

Mind you, they seemed to be doing a little more than

OK at the time, what with a Top Ten album and Top Thirty single!

This success meant Tony Stratton-Smith could no longer cope with both managing the band and being their record company boss at Charisma, so he reluctantly agreed to step down as Genesis' manager. His replacement was Tony Smith, a rock promoter, who had already turned the group down once before. This time he had no doubts.

"We were obviously becoming more and more popular," recalls Phil Collins, "but we didn't have amazing record deals and stuff – we were still only earning about thirty-five pounds a week. Tony saw all this and wanted to try and help us, I think".

Smith immediately arranged for them to tour America again – and this time he went along as well to make sure everything ran smoothly! Despite a few minor problems, the tour was such a success that Bruce Meyer, writing in his syndicated UPI column, called Genesis "the most significant rock band to happen since The Beatles".

But behind the scenes, all was not happy. Peter was beginning to feel more and more isolated from the others, although ironically he'd formed an easy rapport with Phil, who was still in a way one of the 'new boys', despite having now been in the band for four years.

"I felt very easy with Phil. There were times at some gigs when we used to go into a room to get away from it all and sit down together at a piano. My piano playing was humble and, at that point, Phil's was even more humble.

"We used to sing with each other and get into grooves. They were great moments. I think we would both fantasise then about making music on our own, or doing things together."

Because of this, the two of them became close friends, although Pete often looked – in vain – for support that he felt he needed from Phil. "He could be a terrible coward. I had originally asserted a lot of influence over the choice of a new drummer and – at the time – I had felt that I got a sort of soul brother in the band, in terms of feel. When there were arguments, I would look to Phil, as I thought that he would be in support of what I was saying – and he would sit on the fence and refuse to budge."

And so the arguments continued – more out of frustration than contempt. "Genesis was a collaborative venture, a co-operative" stressed Pete. "All the royalties were being split equally and there was a lot of idealism.

"And then, suddenly, I was being singled out as the front man, the performer. I was doing all the interviews and people assumed that I did all the writing. In order to redress the balance, I played down my role.

"I think I had the benefit of the excitement of being the front-man. But the penalty for that was that, within the band, there was a hotbed of resentment towards me, which was never openly declared.

"As a result, I was not treated very sympathetically. In other words, they were less prepared to give me space to do things, as they felt that I'd already got more space than I deserved!"

That summer of 1974, Genesis began work on their most ambitious and courageous project so far – a concept album! Several ideas were considered initially, but these were soon whittled down to just two serious suggestions. Tony was keen to continue the band's flirtation with fantasy and mythology by creating a modern version of 'The Little Prince', a children's fairy story.

Peter was violently opposed to this.

"I thought that was too twee. This was 1974 and I thought we needed to base the story around a contemporary figure rather than a fantasy creation."

To this end, Gabriel came up with a character called Rael, an angry and confused anti-establishment adolescent, a 'West Side Story'-type rebel – in Peter's own words, "this street character in leather jacket and jeans."

Naturally, Mike's initial reaction was disgust. "It's about a greasy Puerto Rican kid!" he exclaimed. But when he'd given the basic premise more consideration, he became quite excited by the challenge ahead.

"For once we were writing about subject matter that was neither airy-fairy or romantic. We finally managed to get away from writing about unearthly things which I think helped the album."

Having persuaded the others to go along with his basic concept, Peter was now faced with another problem: how to tell the rest of the (normally democratic and co-operative) band that he wished to write all the lyrics himself?

"We had all these heavy arguments about writing the lyrics," he recalls. "My argument was that there aren't many novels written by committee. I think I said 'this is something that only I'm going to be able to get into, in terms of understanding the characters and the situations'."

In the end, Peter's intensely personal plea was convincing enough for him to be appointed the sole lyric writer for the recording project which was by now called *The Lamb Lies Down On Broadway*.

Everyone felt quite excited by the depth of the venture; there was a genuine feeling that they were striving to create something radically different. They all moved into Headley Grange mansion (previously occupied by such groups as Led Zeppelin, Bad Company and The Pretty Things) and began writing furiously.

Phil: "We were all living together and writing together and it went very well to start with. Pete had demanded that he do all the words so Mike and Tony had backed off and we were merrily churning out this music. Every time we sat down and played, something good came out."

In no time at all, Phil, Mike, Tony and Steve had written so many new melodies that it was obvious there was too much to go on a normal LP. They were all agreed *The Lamb* would have to be a double album. Everything was going really well until Peter suddenly got a telephone call from Hollywood.

It was William Friedkin, who'd directed the stunning horror success 'The Exorcist'. He'd read the short story that Peter had written on the sleeve of *Genesis Live* and was intrigued.

"He thought it indicted a weird, visual mind" laughs Peter. "Friedkin was trying to put together a sci-fi film and he wanted to get a writer who'd never been involved with Hollywood before."

Gabriel made up his mind almost immediately: he

wanted to go! He tried to break the news to the band gently but they were staggered.

Phil: "Suddenly Peter came up and said 'Do you mind if we stop for a bit?', and we all said 'No – of course we don't want to stop'. It was a matter of principle more than anything else. So he said 'OK, I want to do the film, so I'm leaving'.

"I remember we were sitting in the garden by the porch saying 'What are we going to do? We'll carry on. We'll have an instrumental group', which for five minutes was a serious idea because we had lots of music written."

Peter's announcement caused a lot of resentment within the group and there was strong determination that they should continue with *The Lamb* even if it meant they'd have to come up with a brand new narrative. Pressure mounted – not least because if Friedkin finally offered the job to Gabriel, there would be no room for the rest of the band (in fact, Tangerine Dream had already been contracted to write the film soundtrack).

"Friedkin only wanted me for weird ideas, not for music," explained Peter. "I just wanted a month to do this script outline. So I walked out."

After a week, Peter was back at Headley Grange and work was resumed on the album. "I think Friedkin got frightened at the idea of being the cause of breaking up the group," offers Phil. "He told Pete that he didn't want *that* much of a commitment, just a few ideas. So Pete found himself, from what I can gather, without a job and came back with his tail between his legs. Things were restored to normal but, from that moment on, I think we all felt this could happen again at any time."

There was, however, still one major problem. Peter, distracted by other ambitions, simply hadn't written enough lyrics but refused to let anyone else contribute to the storyline.

"We went to Wales to record," recalls Phil. "We put down the backing tracks and a month later we were still waiting for the words. Then Peter started saying 'I need another piece of music to link these two songs'. We got bored with it all in the end and nobody could help him because he was determined to do it all on his own."

Mike: "It finally became apparent that we hadn't got a chance in hell of getting it finished by the deadline."

It was only then that Peter finally relented and agreed to let the others write some lyrics. "There were two or three holes," says Tony. And so he and Mike wrote 'Carpet Crawlers' and 'Grand Parade Of Lifeless Packaging'.

The finished double album of *The Lamb Lies Down On Broadway* was released in November 1974 to mixed reaction from critics and public alike, although it still reached Number Ten in the LP charts.

Genesis embarked upon a mammoth US tour where they intended to play the whole of *The Lamb* each night, even though the record hadn't yet been released there.

Phil: "We played two hours of completely new music and a couple of tunes which they knew at the end – but by then it was too late."

Mike agreed: "It was a big mistake."

A degree of disillusionment set in, more with the situation than the band itself. Everyone considered what to do for the best, but Pete had the most extreme solution: he announced he was quitting the band completely.

"The pressure was accumulating and I was beginning to dislike myself for what I was doing. I finally cracked in Cleveland."

Tony Smith tried to persuade him to reconsider, but Peter knew this was no time for weak compromises. "There was no room to be flexible – if you were in the band, you were in it 100 per cent: or you were out."

The others were bitterly disappointed but not bitter.

Mike: "Pete's personal life was suffering through touring and constant pressure. Perhaps he felt that *The Lamb* was a good, final statement on which to leave."

Certainly the distorted, lavish and rambling four sides of *The Lamb Lies Down On Broadway*, were in many ways a pinnacle of creativity.

Whether this album acted as a catharsis or whether it drained him too much, after *The Lamb Lies Down On Broadway* Gabriel was convinced he could no longer stay within the confines of a group, any group. There would be no going back.

At the last gig that Gabriel ever played with Genesis – at St. Etienne in France, May 1975 – he saluted the rest of them by playing 'The Last Post' on the oboe.

Tony: "I think for people associated with the group – wives, girlfriends and friends – it was really depressing. It was definitely the end of an era, if not the end of the band."

5

PHIL
THE SINGER

"**A**s soon as Pete said he was leaving, we knew we were going to carry on." – Phil Collins.

It wasn't always so obvious. At the time that Peter told the band he intended to quit, morale in Genesis was at an all-time low and several other members were already seriously considering other ventures.

"We agreed to have a couple of months off after the tour, write some songs, and then meet up to play what we'd written," says Phil.

In truth, though, they weren't even sure if there would still be a band to play any new songs to! Steve Hackett, for instance, had such doubts that he began to write some songs on his own without showing the others.

"I thought at the time 'This could be the beginning of my solo career whether I like it or not.'"

So, during June and July, he hid away in Kingsway Recorders studio working on his solo material. This event seemed to make the others realise there was a problem here that wasn't going to disappear overnight. Eventually both Phil Collins and Mike Rutherford helped out on Steve's album, which he called *Voyage Of The Acolyte*.

"I didn't know whether I was going to come out with a bunch of out-takes or whether it was going to be a whole album. I was just glad to get it done."

Phil Collins, meanwhile, encouraged by the sheer enthusiasm of working on Steve's album as a mere 'hired hand', began to spend much more time drumming with a collaborative effort of some musician friends under the collective name Brand X. The first gig of this outfit took place at the LSE in the autumn.

It was a loose aggregate of jazz-inspired musicians with a feel for contemporary improvisation who had met on a recording project called *The Eddie Howell Gramophone Record.*

As Phil explained "Our tunes are structured in a very loose way, but Brand X started off as a real jamming band in stark contrast to Genesis where we used to tie things down.

"I had been just as responsible for tying things down as everybody else in the band had. Maybe I felt it was something that couldn't change, so I wanted to get out and do something different."

And so, for most of September and October, Phil immersed himself in the recording of the debut Brand X album at London's Trident Studios. It was an all-instrumental jazzy affair called *Unorthodox Behaviour* featuring seven tracks all co-written by the four members of the group: Phil Collins, Percy Jones on bass, Robin Lumley on keyboards and John Goodsall on guitar.

Despite being regarded as minority music, it eventually sold 100,000 copies world-wide and won an award in America as 'the best jazz album to come out of Europe'.

The time that Phil had spent recording and playing with Brand X had given the rest of the members of Genesis time to reconsider the future and perhaps this was just the breathing space that was needed, because in the later summer of 1975, the remaining four members of Genesis – Phil, Steve, Mike and Tony – had got back together and agreed to start work on a new album . . . even though they still hadn't decided what to do about a vocalist.

The band had made a secret agreement with Gabriel that he would delay announcing his departure in order to give Genesis time to reappraise their own future away from the glare of unwelcome publicity.

By the time the band all met up again, they'd already composed enough new material to record another album and so they advertised for someone to replace Peter – and they were overwhelmed by the response: letters, phone calls, even demonstration cassettes!

"It was amazing," laughs Phil. "Some of these people were singing along to Genesis tracks and you could hear the record in the background. Mick Rogers came down from Manfred Mann, but he was basically a guitarist who sang. We only wanted singers. Even Nick Lowe sent a tape in!

"In the end we saw about fifty people. But whenever we liked someone's voice, it was always because it sounded like Pete's. We eventually settled on one bloke we liked and went into the studio with him."

By November, Genesis had already completed several backing tracks of new songs and were ready to begin laying down the overdubs, including the vocals. The first track was 'Squonk' and so this was given to the new vocalist to sing. It was in the wrong key and he was incredibly nervous: so much so, in fact, that Phil walked out of the studio in embarrassment.

"Next day I came in and I said 'Listen I wouldn't mind a crack at it', because deep down I really wanted to have a go. I started to sing the first line, 'Like father, like son . . .' and everybody started to perk up."

Although Phil had sung the occasional song before, no-one had ever regarded him as a bona-fide vocalist. But he handled 'Squonk' with a smoothness and confidence that impressed the others.

Tony: "Phil had a real go at it and it immediately sounded a lot better. Slowly it dawned on us that we weren't going to find another singer, so we decided to let Phil try a couple more."

Suddenly, they'd completed the whole album without having chosen a new vocalist . . . and Phil had sung all the songs!

They were concerned what their record company might think – especially since the band were close to breaking really huge in America and Gabriel had been an important focus to that onslaught – but they needn't have worried.

Tony Stratton-Smith: "When I heard the tapes with Phil singing, I thought they were amazing – he sounded more like Peter Gabriel than Peter Gabriel did!"

The rest of the band were equally delighted.

"We were all very proud of ourselves and pleased that we'd done it as a four-piece," recalls Tony. "It was a very happy album to make. At that time we all felt like underdogs."

But even once the album was completed, with producer Dave Hentschel a guiding light, Genesis continued the search for a new permanent vocalist to replace Peter Gabriel.

"At that point, we still regarded Phil as the drummer," says Mike. "It was never a case of 'Oh good, there's Phil – I hope it'll be OK'. He slowly took on the role of singer on the album, it just happened naturally. I didn't like to suggest Phil as a permanent solution, as I wasn't sure he wanted to give up contact with the drums."

But Phil had indeed been considering just such a move, although he had serious doubts about the whole situation.

"I think it was my wife Andrea who suggested that I take on the singer's role. I said 'No, I'm not going to come out from behind the drums. I like drumming. You must be joking!'

"Anyway, I suggested it to the other guys in the band and, after a while, they thought it wasn't such a silly idea. That meant I had to find another drummer."

He approached Bill Bruford, who had already been the drummer for two of Britain's top 'progressive' outfits – Yes and King Crimson. He was presently involved with the Brand X project, playing percussion while Phil took care of the drums.

One day, during a break in rehearsals with Brand X, Phil casually mentioned that Gabriel had left and he was considering taking over the vocal duties himself.

Bruford thought it was a great idea and immediately said "You sing and I'll play drums!" This was just what Phil was hoping for – "I had admired Bill's playing for years" – but had been too nervous to ask.

So Bruford joined the band on a temporary basis, while Genesis considered the future: did Phil continue as vocalist or did they look for a permanent replacement for

Gabriel, and did Phil give up playing the drums or not?

In the meantime, in February 1976 they quelled all the 'Genesis are dead' headlines by releasing *Trick Of The Tail*, their seventh studio album and their biggest seller so far. By March, it had reached Number Three in the albums chart.

It was also a landmark for their songwriting. Until now, all the material on Genesis records had been credited as joint compositions, but the public took this to mean that Gabriel, as the public face of the band, had been responsible for the majority of it. (In fact, he'd written very little music and – apart from *The Lamb Lies Down On Broadway* – only half of the lyrics.) And so, to give credit where credit is due, from *A Trick Of The Tail* onwards, song-writing credits were shown individually.

Of the eight tracks on that album, Phil Collins helped write only three: 'Robbery, Assault and Battery', which he wrote with Tony Banks, plus 'Los Endos' and 'Dance On A Volcano' which were both group efforts.

To capitalise on the success of *A Trick*, Genesis returned to North America for a huge tour, and here it was – at London, Ontario in Canada – that Phil Collins made his debut as the group's lead singer.

"I remember going to the first gig scared stiff, not about the singing – but the communication with the audience, always one of Pete's strong points. He used to tell these funny stories between each song, which amused the crowd and covered up a lot of tuning and instrument changes.

"But as soon as I'd started, the audience was so warm they must have known how nervous we were all feeling. After the first tune, everything settled down and it was fine.

"My first stipulation when I agreed to take over was to do it my own way and not have to pick up where Peter left off. I just wanted to sing and you simply couldn't do that properly in the sort of costumes we had for *The Lamb Lies Down On Broadway*.

"I didn't mind if there was a song where I could assume a role unselfconsciously – like in 'Robbery, Assault And

Battery' where I used to put on a jacket and a hat: just like the Dodger! Or 'Say It's Alright Joe', where I was a drunk in a bar – I could relate to that!

"After a while people started saying 'How come your voice sounds lot like Pete's?' But I wasn't actually trying to make it sound like anybody.

"If there were any harmonies involved on our albums, it was usually me singing them. And on some of the songs like 'I Know What I Like', there were usually two voices singing all the time. You got used to the sound of our vocals, so if you took half away, the other sounded very similar. My voice was there, but people always thought it was Pete's."

The rest of the band were delighted with the way Phil had grown into the role of singer on stage. "Phil was a more natural singer than Pete," reckons Tony. "Pete was more contrived as a singer. I've always loved Pete's voice, but I wished that he would let his voice be more natural. But Phil has a very pure voice which has got better and better over the years."

Phil himself was in no doubt as to why the audiences accepted him so quickly. "I think they see me as more of a regular bloke; without the mysterious, remote qualities that Pete had. I think it's nice when you can crack a joke and make yourself look an idiot. It deflates any kind of pomp."

At last Phil had stepped out from the shadows. He was a born performer and used all the theatrical experience he'd gained as a child to full advantage.

The American tour was followed by a trek through Europe as the band become more successful than ever. "Finally," says press agent Peter Thompson, "the media picked up on them. You could actually say something about them in the kind of daily newspapers that my mother reads – not just the rock papers."

Confident and buoyant in the wake of having re-established themselves without the dramatic presence of Gabriel, Genesis came back to Britain for a brief rest – during which time Phil played a few more gigs with Brand X – before leaving for Hilvarenbeek in Holland to record a new album, *Wind And Wuthering*, which they all approached with a seriousness bordering on solemnity.

"We all stayed in this little house," recalls Phil, "all boys together! There were no ladies around. We just concentrated on the job in hand."

Mainly "the job in hand" consisted of arranging and rehearsing material that had already been written.

"Tony had written a couple of songs," says Phil. "Mike had a couple and I chipped in here and there. I wasn't too involved with it – I did the best I could but I didn't feel that it was a true representation of what I wanted to do. I found that I wasn't writing much. Something wasn't quite right."

By contrast, Tony Banks regarded the *Wind And Wuthering* album as the best so far: "It's definitely the most musically complex and it has a mysterious quality to it. You needed to hear it several times before you could fully appreciate it."

But while Tony Banks had contributed to most of the album's nine tracks, guitarist Steve Hackett was involved with only two – even though he'd written others which he regarded as his best songs ever.

"There was a track of mine called 'Please Don't Touch' which was going to be on the album, as the whole band were keen on it. One day, in rehearsal, Phil said 'Can't get behind that' – and we dropped it! I wrote another song called 'Hoping Love Will Last'. I felt the band were incapable of performing it and it was eventually recorded by Randy Crawford.

"I said to Phil one day 'I've written one of the best things I've ever done'. And he said 'solo material?' and I said 'Yeah'. It was at that point that he knew how dissatisfied I was.

"I felt that the band was starting to repeat itself; we weren't really exploring enough new areas . . . maybe I felt confused because my life seemed to be outlined for the next year. We had seven months of touring coming up and I didn't really know if I was going to enjoy it. I would really rather have done a solo album."

While Hackett was considering his future, Genesis were surprised to learn that Bill Bruford had decided to leave after just a year.

Phil: "We read in Melody Maker that Bill was joining a group with Rick Wakeman and John Wetton. I rang him and said 'Are you with them or are you staying with us?' and he said 'Ah, I meant to tell you about that!'."

Bill, for his part, regarded it as a natural progression: "I always considered my time with Genesis as temporary, although the group were very friendly and never actually asked me to leave. It was just that I wanted to move on to something else."

Bill's departure left Genesis requiring a new drummer to play on the forthcoming tours of Britain and America. They chose Chester Thompson, who had previously played with not only Frank Zappa and the Pointer Sisters, but also with Weather Report – one of Phil Collin's all-time favourite groups.

"I knew straight away that Chester was the right guy – I wanted to make sure we had someone with impeccable taste and class. I couldn't find someone better to play with than him. Perhaps this was due to the fact that at that time I was very influenced by black music."

And so, on several songs, Genesis fans could now witness the spectacle of both Phil and Chester flailing away in unison.

"We decided to work something out together. There are two examples of two drummers that I can think of, which are perfect – one is Joe Cocker's Mad Dogs and Englishmen when they had Jim Keltner and Jim Gordon and the other is Zappa live on the *Roxy And Elsewhere* album with Chester and Ralph Humphrey . . . and that's what made me think of Chester because there's one song called 'More Trouble Every Day' when they do this lick together which we've done in our songs too because it's such a great lick. It's a unison thing – as I said before, it's a great discipline."

Chester's background in jazz and soul gave Genesis a new lease of life, pumping a greater rhythmic urgency into old songs like 'Eleventh Earl Of Mar'. This new-found vitality was much in evidence on the band's huge tour of 1977, which started in England before encompassing the USA (headlining at Madison Square Garden in New York and The Forum in Los Angeles), South America (football stadiums in Rio and Sao Paulo) and Europe, where they played five sell-out concerts at the Palais Des Sports in Paris, recording the proceedings for a second live album, the cleverly-titled *Seconds Out*.

But while the band were mixing the live versions for release, Steve Hackett announced he was definitely leaving. The others were shocked, because they thought that Hackett's dissatisfaction over how many of his own songs could be accepted in Genesis had been solved by recording a solo album. Or, as Phil Collins told NME at the time: "Steve could have done everything he's doing now – and still stayed in Genesis!"

But Hackett wanted more; he wanted true equal shares, a quarter of all Genesis songs to be written by him.

"We just don't do things like that," said Phil. "We use the best material that's around. Steve, unfortunately, didn't write songs that appealed to everybody as much as Mike and Tony did – I thought his frustration at that time seemed unreasonable, but at the same time, understandable.

"But we'd always worked on songs that motivated everybody rather than 'I want a quarter of the album'. It was weird, I didn't feel emotional when he left. It had been very different when Pete left."

Hackett's departure prompted the title of the band's next album. *And Then There Were Three* (even though the nucleus of Collins-Rutherford-Banks had already been augmented for live concerts by not only Chester Thompson but also bassist Daryl Stuermer), with Phil again singing and Mike playing all the guitar parts.

Released in April 1978 and again recorded in Holland, this album demonstrated that Genesis were moving into a new phase of modern melodicism – "It was a challenge to see if we could just write some nice songs that stood up," explained Phil diplomatically. "We tried to be more concise with the tunes."

But still the feelings of doubt that had dogged him on *Wind And Wuthering* persisted on *And Then There Were Three*.

"It's not one of my favourite albums," he admits. "I can't put my finger on why it isn't. I don't understand it at all."

Nevertheless, it was regarded by the public as a huge success and even spawned the band's first-ever Top Ten hit single in 'Follow You Follow Me'.

And so the success story became a bandwagon with its own momentum. One hit album followed another, just as each sell-out tour was better than the last. In August Genesis played the huge Knebworth Fair (just north of London) watched by 100,000 rapt fans. A month later they played in front of 120,000 fans at the Fête de L'Humanité in Paris.

At this stage, the band were becoming more and more remote from the fans who had come to see them. The vast auditoria necessary to hold everyone who wanted tickets were cavernous venues providing very little warmth or intimacy. A communication barrier was being erected, slowly and invisibly but with inevitable certainty.

The Genesis show began to rely more and more on extravagant light shows and awesome sound systems, so much so that the band were almost trapped by the same problem that threatened to engulf them when Gabriel was dazzling the fans with his costume changes: no-one really noticed any more how well the band were actually playing!

After a particularly gruelling tour of Japan – and three separate tours of America – Genesis made a conscious decision to scale down the shows and revert to playing smaller venues where they could talk directly to the fans.

But by now, the external difficulties were dwarfed by internal disaster and the band came close to splitting up when Phil's marriage to Andrea collapsed under the strain of constant pressure and commitments to Genesis.

"Mike and I felt very strongly that the best thing was to step back and let Phil sort it out," recalls Tony. "The last thing that he wanted was endless sympathy from us."

Nobody knew what was really going on. The future – for Phil Collins as a husband and Genesis as a group – looked decidedly bleak. In fact, it seemed like the end for both of them.

6

BREAKING UP IS HARD TO DO. . .

Phil Collins had met Andrea Bertorelli while they were both studying at the Barbara Speake Stage School. She was a pretty young actress who had appeared in West End theatre productions of 'The Prime Of Miss Jean Brodie' and 'Maggie May' and he'd been courting her on and off for about six years before they were eventually married in 1975.

They had two children – a little boy, Simon, born in September 1976 and an adopted daughter, Joely – and if you were to ask any of their friends, you'd be told that Phil and Andrea were a very happily married couple.

At least, up until New Year's Eve 1978: this was when Phil announced "I've got to go on the road next year, Genesis has to crack America."

And Andrea replied "Well, then we're not going to be together in twelve months' time."

Phil readily understood her anxiety at the prospect of spending a whole year alone, but hoped that if he could just get through the gruelling schedule of the next twelve months, then the subsequent global success that Genesis should achieve would allow him some precious breathing space and he'd be able to take some time off to become a family man again.

But for the present, Phil prayed that Andrea would be patient for just a little while longer. The needs of the band – who were on the very brink of major American success and needed just one more push – seemed more immediately urgent.

"I thought 'I have to do it, I can't let the boys down' – not realising that I was one of the boys and I could say something about it. I just asked her to bear with me for one more year. 'It'll be all right'."

But it wasn't all right.

"She could see it coming because she was one of those people who didn't like being alone. In the same way as you find someone who hates spiders and you put them in a room full of them, you can't say 'They're only spiders, they won't hurt you'. I was saying to Andrea, 'Just another month', but she didn't like being alone . . . and I was leaving her by herself a lot."

In fact, the ironic element of those Genesis tours to America was that they had been specifically designed so that none of the band had to be away from home for months on end at any one time, but it didn't really work out like that, as Mike explained: "We had this crazy idea to do America in three short tours, rather than do one long tour.

"What we didn't realise was that going there and back six times made it seem much longer."

By the time Phil returned from the tour, it wasn't America that was cracking, but his marriage – Andrea was having an affair with another man.

"I remember it all vividly: all rationality seemed to go out of the window then. I came back from the third American tour and the first night I slept in the spare room. It was that bad.

"I just couldn't believe that this bloke that I'd got in to decorate my house had actually gone off with my wife. I think it happened because I was working such a lot – I was always doing something, if it wasn't Genesis, it was Brand X and if it wasn't Brand X, it was a session – and although we tried to move closer together, we just moved further and further apart. Then I had to go away to Japan. Maybe I should have cancelled the tour.

"But, no, I went to Japan – and spent ten days drunk. I hated every minute of it. I couldn't sing and everyone was concerned about my welfare, although there was nothing anyone could do about it."

When he came back from Japan, Phil and Andrea sat down to discuss the possibility of a reconciliation. What they needed was a fresh start away from it all – so they agreed to sell the house and move to Vancouver, where Andrea's mother lived.

"I had dinner with Tony, Mike and Tony Smith and I said 'Listen, if you don't mind coming to Vancouver to record, then we've still got a group. But if you can't, then this is the end'.

"So I went over there, looked around at a few houses and thought 'OK, I'll do my album now and leave the group'. Then it suddenly dawned on me that the marriage was no better than it had been in England."

Phil said goodbye to his wife and returned to England to see what he could salvage of Genesis, only to discover that while he had been away, the group had ceased to function as a working unit and Tony and Mike had concentrated their efforts on solo recording projects.

Phil came back home to Guildford and sunk into a deep depression. Later, he rationalised the split to friends: "My marriage broke up simply because I was working too hard. I don't do much in my spare time apart from music. My wife began to regard music as the other woman – for her, it was like me having a mistress."

To Phil, it wasn't like that at all. "I didn't see music as causing it." And ironically, Andrea herself had been the one to encourage Phil to dive headlong into the melting pot of responsibility by suggesting that he take over the Genesis vocals after Peter had left. If only she'd known then . . .

Of course the constant pressure of pop at the top – the long hours in the studio, the months on tour, the hectic schedules – has an inevitable toll of its own and for Phil and Andrea, it had become an unbearable price to pay for success. During 1978, Genesis had been on tour virtually non-stop – three trips to America and one to Japan. The pressure had built up until a split was almost unavoidable.

"I think it happened because I was working such a lot – and although we tried to move closer together, we just moved further and further apart. Situations like that are always painful.

"I was asked what aspect of the divorce most upset me. And it was that someone I thought loved me, apparently didn't any more. I had known my wife since schooldays, and I went out with her on and off since I was thirteen . . . but if you feel that a relationship is no good anymore, then that's the only way to handle it."

Suddenly he was all alone in a big empty house, surrounded by the memories of the two most important things in his life: his family and his music.

He felt utterly alone – discarded almost – and the greatest irony was that it was the incessant pressure of work that had put such an intolerable strain on his marriage, causing it to break down . . . and yet now that he was all alone with no family around him, he didn't even have any work to take his mind off the emotional turmoil in his head.

Genesis was in a state of suspension until Tony Banks and Mike Rutherford finished working on their solo albums (*A Curious Feeling* and *Smallcreep's Day* respectively), while Brand X – unable to wait until there was a convenient gap in Phil's hectic work schedule – had set off on a world tour without him.

Faced with a cold, uncomfortable empty void, he began writing songs.

It was almost as though Phil Collins had chanced upon the advice given to F Scott Fitzgerald by Ernest Hemingway: "You have to be hurt like hell before you can write seriously. But when you get the damned hurt, use it – don't cheat with it."

The first songs Phil began writing by himself were wracked with pain and bitterness and guilt and love turned cold. They were a turning-point in both his personal and professional life.

Phil had never been a prolific composer at all – he'd had neither the time nor inspiration to attempt it seriously. Of course, he had written the odd song here and there: notably 'Space Child' for the Flaming Youth album and 'Lily-White Lilith' on *The Lamb Lies Down On Broadway* (even though it was actually credited as a group effort).

Admittedly, he'd always been involved with finishing the songs off or suggesting original ideas – "I mean, I've got lots of bits of songs, don't get me wrong; 'Ballad Of Big' is mainly mine, bits of 'Down And Out' are mine . . ." – but he'd always lacked the total dedication and solitude to sit down with a blank sheet of paper and come up with a finished composition.

"I'd never really finished a song until I was on my own, in '78-'79. I just had this year of writing all these songs, basically because I was depressed, miserable, and I wanted to try and get my family together again. I used to go upstairs and cry my eyes out . . .

"And also, suddenly I realised I could do it, because suddenly I had the *time* to do it. Before that, I was just playing, and then the family and taking the dog for walks, and then playing.

"When I was here with the wife and the kids, between Genesis, Brand X and other sessions I wanted to do, I felt obliged – quite rightly, I suppose – to not go up there and lock myself away and write.

"But when they're not here, you haven't got much else to do – and obviously it was depressing . . . so it wasn't until my marriage broke up that I found the time – or had the time, not found it – to write . . . and also the emotional inclination to sit at a piano and pour my heart out, which is what I did on the first songs that I wrote.

"It's sad that you have to experience pain to be an artist . . . I think human beings generally wallow in being miserable. I think it's curious that if you're unhappy, you don't put on a happy record to lift you out of it – in nine cases out of ten, you'll put a sad record on the stereo and have a wonderfully depressing time.

"I suppose this might sound funny, but I think I almost enjoyed being miserable. Many songs just seem to come out when you're depressed and wallowing in self-pity.

"And I did wallow . . . I wasn't enjoying it, but at the same time it was a very stimulating year to go through in that respect. I mean, every time I started to do something, words and music came out at the same time; words that were actually – depending on whether you actually like them or not – I thought, very, very strong.''

The song titles of those early songs reflected Phil's fragile, over-emotional moods dramatically, almost bitterly – 'Don't Let Him Steal Your Heart Away', 'Why Can't It Wait Until Morning', 'Misunderstanding'.

''If someone gave me the choice – if they had said that in ten years' time I would either be doing this or I would still be with my family, there's no way I would have said I'd rather be doing this. I would have said I'd rather be with my family.

''I'm not afraid to say 'I love you' in a song – or even to make myself look a bit of a wally. People ask whether I get embarrassed revealing my private thoughts and emotions in a song and maybe looking a bit soft – but I don't. Not at all.''

After a period of soul-searching, Phil had got rid of a lot of his bitterness and depression through the catharsis of expressing himself in his songs: at last he felt able to venture out of his self-imposed exile.

In April 1979, Phil went off into the country to Startling Studios in Ascot to record new material for *Product* – the fifth Brand X album. He'd appeared on the first two studio LPs as well as the *Livestock* live album, but 1978's *Masques* had been recorded and released while Phil was on the Japanese leg of the Genesis world tour. But now he was back – and eager to blow away the cobwebs.

''We had two weeks booked twenty-four hours a day solid with two engineers and two line-ups – two separate groups, one working during the day and the other through the night.

''We'd be having dinner while the others were just getting up for breakfast! We had a great time!''

After Tony and Mike had finished all the work on their solo projects, all three members of Genesis got back together once more, meeting up at Phil's house to rehearse for what might be their last-ever album. And everything just clicked into place!

''Suddenly the jams worked again,'' says Tony Banks. '' 'Duchess', 'Behind The Lines' and 'Turn It On Again' were written by us all together. I felt it was more rewarding than just writing a lot of songs individually. We couldn't have carried on with Mike and I writing the bulk of the material. There wouldn't have been much in it for Phil if we had carried on that way."

This was something that Phil himself had already come to realise – but it had taken something as dramatic as a broken marriage to act as a catalyst.

"It was only then that I had finished songs that I could put to the band: Tony and Mike had been the most prolific writers in the band in recent years and so I just put bits in and Tony and Mike would add something to it somewhere and it would be a group song.

"So I played Genesis 'In The Air Tonight' and 'If Leaving Me Is Easy', but they were kind of too simple for the band – I'm glad the others didn't want to include 'In The Air Tonight', as I'm sure it wouldn't have ended up sounding the way I wanted it to.

"But I played them oceans of stuff – I had an awful lot of songs that were not really Genesis-ey, but 'Misunderstanding' was one of my songs which they liked, it was a song that everybody liked and we didn't change it. It was meant to be a song that anybody could listen to – not just Genesis fans – a song about a girl meeting a boy.

"And they liked 'Please Don't Ask', which was a very personal lyric." But Mike and Tony certainly didn't accept everything that Phil played them.

"I wrote some words to 'Behind The Lines' which I'm glad we didn't use. I started singing them and everybody said 'You can't sing that!' We were getting a lot of flak from the music press at the time and I had written these pretty cynical lyrics which Tony and Mike were a bit embarrassed by."

One of the problems – for Genesis at least – with Phil's songs was that he'd written on the keyboards. Now, as even Phil will admit, he's no pianist. But when the classically-trained Tony Banks tried to play the same melodies, they sounded not only completely different, but also . . . somehow not quite right!

"I have a certain amount of technique, but certainly not

a keyboard player's technique," explains Phil. "I had an aunt who was a piano teacher, and she was capable of teaching me far more than I wanted to be taught, but I didn't really gain that much knowledge.

"If you don't know the rules you don't know whether you're breaking them or not. If you do something, you just do it because it sounds nice."

Out of perhaps a dozen songs that Phil had finished, he'd played Genesis about half to be considered for inclusion on the new group LP (by then entitled *Duke*) – and they'd accepted just two!

"We ended up with the situation that I had written my collection of songs – and Tony and Mike had done their solo albums, so we all played each other little bits we had . . . and we didn't have that much!

Taking Phil's two songs – 'Misunderstanding' and 'Please Don't Ask' – plus another couple from Tony and one from Mike, Genesis still didn't have even half an album's worth of new material after a two year gap since their previous record.

"So we started writing from scratch," recalls Phil, "which is what the band does best and what we used to do but got out of the habit of doing around the period of *And Then There Were Three.*

"It's down to the three of us sparking ideas off each other. And it is interesting, because we're all from different backgrounds – well, Tony and Mike are from similar backgrounds, but I'm from a very different background to them and those two guys are very different from each other. "So we throw pieces of music around . . . like 'Turn It On Again' was a riff of Mike's and because I was really listening to a lot of Earth Wind & Fire at the time, I said 'Listen, I can see it this way . . .', so I took it a lot up in tempo and Mike said 'I never thought of that!', so there's that spark – and that's what's great about being in the group!

"Up until recently with the band, if anything was simple it would be 'Let's complicate it a bit', whereas I'd prefer to simplify it even more."

Although several of Phil's solo compositions had been

rejected by the group mainly because they were too personal emotionally, it was, in fact, the intense personal nature of the lyrics that set *Duke* apart from the previous Genesis albums, as Tony is quick to concede. "I felt by the time we got to *Duke*, Phil was actually projecting his own personality into our songs. That's what a good singer should do."

Duke was released in March 1980 heralding a brave new stand for Genesis, yet no-one seemed to notice the shift in emphasis, either musically or lyrically.

"I was very upset at some of the reviews of *Duke*," spits Phil, "because a lot of time and energy went into it and I felt closer to *Duke* than any other album that Genesis has done but that was because I had the time and wasn't married any more. I had the time to be in the studio first and leave last.

"So I was annoyed that people thought they could dismiss it in six paragraphs. It's my sincere belief that Genesis have become more accessible down the years. We produce very fine albums and singles.

"You see, there are people out there who should have heard *Duke* and would have liked it but they weren't really given the chance. People need an excuse. They give Peter Gabriel the benefit of the doubt but not Genesis. With Peter, they've had the chance to reassess. You have to spell it out."

The band set off on yet another major British tour, this time concentrating on smaller halls including Aylesbury Friars, scene of many of their earliest triumphs.

Meanwhile, 'Misunderstanding' – virtually Phil's first solo composition for the group – became Genesis' first US Top Ten single and the band capitalised on their sudden popularity with another massive US tour.

During this tour of America, Phil met Jill Tavelman, a Californian teacher. They fell in love at first sight and according to Armando Gallo's excellent Genesis book, "his performances improved day by day".

"She didn't know who I was when we met, so it was totally honest," says Phil. At last, all the tears of bitterness were beginning to melt away.

7

FACE VALUE

Returning home from the Genesis tour of America, Phil scorned the chance of a few weeks' rest on a beach somewhere tropical, preferring instead to lock himself away in an upstairs bedroom which had been converted into a studio, with one wall covered in gold and platinum Genesis records.

It was in his little room at home that Phil worked out the rest of the songs that Genesis hadn't used for *Duke*: some of them were just basic ideas, others had snatches of lyric. All of them were intensely personal. "The way that it first started was that I'd written the songs – and then I was just stuck with this bunch of depressing songs that I needed to record.

"So I put them on eight-track and they were demos; demos of something that might be recorded at some point in the future. I needed to indulge myself in something just to help myself forget."

But before he could forget, Phil first had to relive the breakdown of his marriage through the lyrics of the songs written at the height of his despair. It was almost like a ritual exorcism, a primal exercise in fully understanding the pain and jealousy and guilt by immersing himself in the trauma of that emotional tornado all over again.

The lyrics laid all the torment and betrayal bare with lines like:

'I wish that I could write you a love song

To tell you how I feel
It seems you don't like to listen . . .'

from 'You Know What I Mean' and

'So you finally came right out and said it, girl
What took you so long?
It was in your eyes
And that look's been there for far too long'

from 'I Missed Again', and even more graphically, the
following verse from 'If Leaving Me Is Easy':

'You're gone now,
But your heart still remains,
And it'll be here if you come again . . .'

"I was just writing songs as messages," said Phil. "I
really felt I'd been hard done by – and so did Andrea. I
never felt bad about talking about myself or revealing
myself that publicly on a record. A lot of people don't like
to say those things, even to a friend, let alone to millions of
record-buyers. But I never really thought about it: it's
about feelings, so any songs should be as disturbing as the
emotions involved."

But by now, Phil had already found a new love in his
life, American Jill Tavelman, and this prompted him to
say, "If 'In The Air Tonight' reflects my past relationship,
then 'This Must Be Love' certainly reflects my hope for the
future."

And certainly lines such as 'Happiness is something I
thought I'd never feel again/But now I know/It's you I've
been looking for' suggested that Phil's future would be
very bright indeed!

The rough demonstration versions of these songs consisted of sparse arrangements recorded very simply –
mainly just keyboards for the melodies, with the rhythm
maintained by a Roland drum-machine – admittedly a
strange method of keeping the beat for a drummer.

"It's convenience really" he explains. "When I first

started recording at home, I said 'No way, I'm a drummer – I don't need a drum-machine!' So I'd sing the song and play the drums, and then I'd go to the piano. And of course, that way the tempo was all over the place."

"Eventually I said 'Okay, I'll try it'. I used it because it freed my writing. Not being able to get from one chord to another very quickly – because of my limited keyboard technique – it gave me time to think about where I was going to go next, having a drum rhythm in the background."

Phil hadn't, at that time, regarded these rough recordings as the blueprint for a solo album; they were just demos of his own songs for his own satisfaction. "So it kinda crept up on me – it wasn't a case of me saying 'I'm going to do a solo album'."

That idea only arose when Ahmet Ertegun – head of Atlantic Records – heard the tapes and immediately said "You've got an album there".

A solo album was something Phil had never previously considered – after all, he was the singer for Genesis!

"The only reason I started doing this stuff at all," he conceded, "was because of the divorce and I just ended up with a lot of time on my hands to write. The songs had been around for a year or two and eventually there were enough I had confidence in. I just thought it was about time I did some songs exactly the way I wanted to.

"If I was still where I was family-wise, maybe I would have done a solo album eventually – but it would've been a little more like a fusion thing. Maybe if I hadn't done it for three or four years, I would have been off that area of music and I'd have tried to do something with singing, but my songs might have been totally different."

But once he'd made the decision to go ahead with the solo project, he was faced with the difficult task of turning rough ideas into finished tracks, or – in his own words – 'polishing up the demos'.

"I suddenly thought 'What if I was to use these tapes as my masters?' – because everyone always talks about how you can never recreate the demo – so we used the tapes, and I took them into the studio and copied my eight-track onto twenty-four-track, leaving sixteen spare tracks to overdub on. So I'd already done the backing tracks and suddenly my album was already half-made."

Then Phil began working on recording the extra instruments – guitar, bass, some extra keyboards, a mournful saxophone for one track and a tearful string section for others, plus of course the drums! – and arranging for various musicians of undoubted calibre to drop by his studio.

Or as Phil offered in a casual manner: "I just got my mates in really to play specific roles."

These 'mates' included such acclaimed musicians as Ronnie Scott, Stephen Bishop, Daryl Stuermer, Peter Robinson, Arif Mardin and even Eric Clapton!

The whole project was approached very much like a mosaic, with Phil carefully fitting together each individual piece in his little studio upstairs in order to create a harmonious finished product.

"Mind you, I had to go to Los Angeles to record some of the people, so I did the vocals there as well!" he laughs, well aware that he's shattering the myth of the 'home-made' product.

"Because I did the recording piece-meal, I could go back and re-record drum parts or whatever. I had two bass players – John Giblin and Alphonso Johnson – but both of them did the same songs and then I just chose the best one.

"If you're recording piece by piece, you just stop as soon as it starts sounding good. Or if it's not working out, you can just knock it on the head and forget about it and maybe come back the next day, which I did an awful lot.

"But I didn't want it to sound too clinical – I wanted to keep that spirit in the music even if that meant I lost out on quality.

"And if you lose a bit of sound quality it doesn't matter, because you're going to gain on emotion anyway. I can't really complain if people don't like it, because that's really what I wanted it to sound like.

"With 'This Must Be Love' or 'In The Air Tonight', I could have put a lot more stuff in there and I guess it's just a case of knowing where to stop. Just like playing instruments, you have to leave some space."

He briefly considered drafting in a 'name' producer to help ensure the sound would be perfect and he drew up a list of his favourite studio wizards: Phil Ramone, Mutt Lange, Maurice White, George Clinton, George Martin . . .

"No, I didn't think of George Martin – if I had, he may have produced it, because I loved the Beatles and he's one of my biggest heroes. I could have had any producer I wanted, at a price. But I had a very strong idea of what I wanted to do myself . . . but those were the sort of people I was thinking about.

"And then suddenly it just came to me, why not do it myself? To me – I've used this before but it puts it in perspective – it's like an artist sitting down in front of a blank canvas and saying to someone else 'Can you put a bit of blue there and a bit of red down there?'.

"You don't do that, you do it yourself – otherwise it's an interpretation. So I would much rather do everything myself."

All of the decisions about who would play what – not to mention how, where and when – rested with Phil alone. He was determined to make the album as 'personal' as possible, and that would be highly unlikely if he had to compromise certain gut feelings to accommodate the style of a producer. "I don't like people telling me what to do," he admitted candidly. "I like things to fit in with my way of thinking. But I didn't so much produce my album as direct it."

One of the major surprises was that Phil's long awaited solo album simply didn't sound like a drummer's record! There's an element of his drumming fitting in more with the songs rather than just being impressive, expressive drumming for the sake of it.

"For the first time," he boasted, "I can say 'This is my album – if you don't like this, you don't like me!' It's a song album rather than a jazz-rock album or a drummer's album."

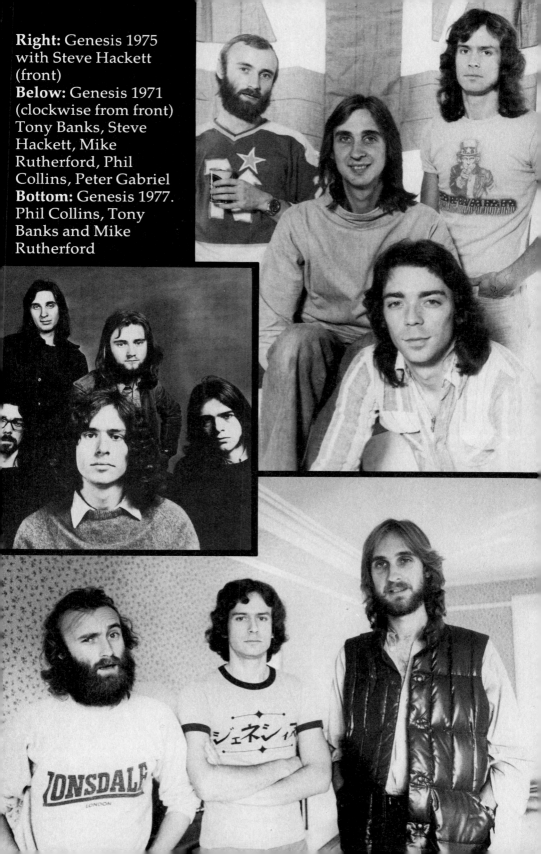

Right: Genesis 1975 with Steve Hackett (front)
Below: Genesis 1971 (clockwise from front) Tony Banks, Steve Hackett, Mike Rutherford, Phil Collins, Peter Gabriel
Bottom: Genesis 1977. Phil Collins, Tony Banks and Mike Rutherford

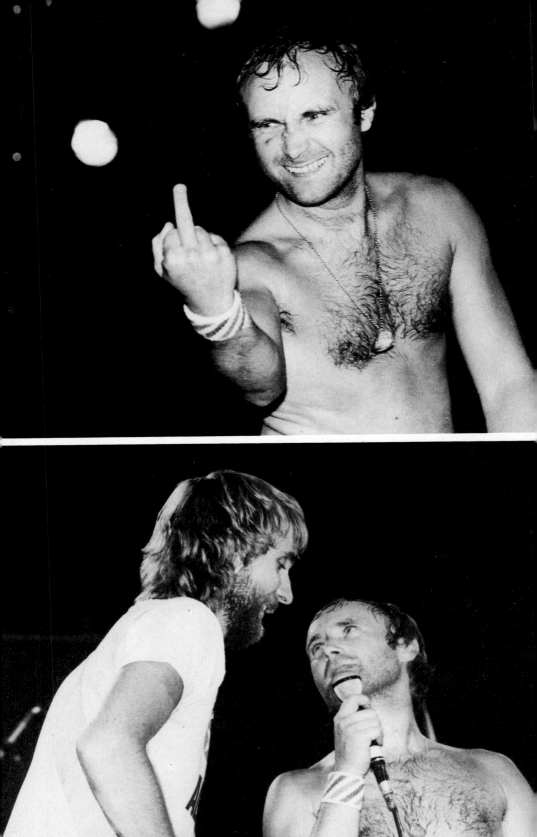

Far left: Genesis at Forest Hills, New York, 1982
Left and below: "I close my eyes and count to ten . . ."

Above: The T-shirt says Brand X, but the banner says solo artist
Below: Thru these walls
Right: The little drummer boy

Above: "Nice little place you've got here . . ."
Below: Upstairs, in a converted bedroom – this is where 'Against All Odds' and 'In The Air Tonight' were born
Right: "Don't let him steal your heart away . . ."

Right: Happy
Together: Phil and his
wife, Jill
Below: Phil with
Robert Plant, New
York

To some people though – especially Genesis fans – it seemed as though Phil were taking quite a few risks, both musically and career-wise.

"I don't think about it in terms of taking risks," he told Paul Morley in an NME interview. "To be honest, something like 'In The Air Tonight' is as simple as hitting a chord and thinking, 'Well, what sounds good coming after that? That'll sound nice coming next...' so it's just interesting for me to do it. I don't take gambles or anything, I just follow my nose a bit.

"I mean, the lyric to 'In The Air Tonight' was improvised, as was the tune, it just came out, I set up a nice tempo and the chords flowed – the words are kind of bitter, I guess, but they're not really related to my domestic situation."

The highly distinctive sound of a song such as 'In The Air Tonight' – the booming drums and dry vocal – was the creation of engineer Hugh Padgham, whom Phil had met when they both worked on Peter Gabriel's third solo album in 1980.

"I don't know the reason why it worked so well. Hugh is a wonderful engineer – he can make a few instruments sound very large. When I worked with Peter and Hugh on getting drum sounds, Peter didn't want any cymbals on the album at all. It was an interesting idea and I went along with it because it was *his* album.

"It's very hard not to be influenced by things you like," he says, "and I do like Peter's music a lot."

In fact, Phil was so mesmerised by Gabriel's desire for sparseness that when the time came to record drums over his basic rhythm tracks, he deliberately tried to recreate for his solo album exactly the same environment by using the same studio – The Townhouse in London – and same engineer – Hugh Padgham.

"I had a very distinct idea of what I wanted the record to sound like and ninety-nine per cent of it came out the way I wanted.

"Hugh and I worked on different sounds for different tracks – very dry for 'This Must be Love' and really huge for 'In The Air Tonight'. On 'I Missed Again', we went for a Tamla Motown sound – and got the old bathroom sound and then it didn't really matter if the cymbals were splashing around – just different things for different tracks really."

This insistence on making each track highly individual merely enhanced the over-all style of Phil's solo creation. The use of banjo on one track and saxophone on another marked the album down as a record radically different from anything expected from a member of Genesis.

"I've been theorising quite a lot about this," said Phil at the time of the album's release, "and I admit that it's easy to theorise when you have a safe commodity behind you like I have.

"But if someone brings out a solo record, in theory if someone buys that record they ought to be able to see where that person is at; liking it or disliking it and therefore liking or disliking the person.

"There's really no other reason for doing it unless you can say 'This is me'. Even if you can't play the instrument yourself, you can guide someone and direct them the way you want it to be.

"From that angle, there is nothing I would change on this album really. It's not often you can say that. You never have the definitive mix . . . and we kept on mixing all the tracks right up until the time when the album was due out!"

Phil's determination to make this record a truly personal statement extended to the sleeve design, which he wanted to make as informal as possible. His reasoning was that he wanted people to appreciate him – and his problems, emotions and fears – as an individual, rather than merely one-third of the still rather faceless supergroup Genesis.

And so the front cover shot was a close-up black-and-white portrait of Phil's face, deliberately chosen for its harsh colourless effect. The back sleeve was a matching photo of the back of Phil's own head featuring the songwriting credits in Phil's own handwriting.

It was a brave attempt at breaking down many of the barriers between performer and audience. But, as ever, several people chose to misinterpret his good intentions.

"That cover picture with a fully frontal view of my luscious features is a very important part of the album, which was, after all, virtually a diary. So – for the cover – I wanted that really close-up photo, to show myself unadorned, as a sort of 'get inside my head' idea.

"As Genesis, I don't think we ever reveal our personalities visually to any great extent. We never put our picture on the album covers because we thought we looked just like any other group. We always went for things that just looked good as a cover. Mind you, some of them – like *Nursery Cryme* or *Foxtrot* – don't look so good now!"

"So that's why my cover is a full-face shot. And when I came to write the credits on the back cover, instead of putting 'Phil Collins' or 'Phil', I put 'me' – but I was criticised for that; it was 'too egotistical'. I mean, Christ you can't win!"

Coming up with a title for the LP was almost more complex than the song-writing itself, as he wanted both to reflect the trauma and emotional turmoil of the previous year. At first he considered *Exposure* to make it obvious that the lyrics were deeply personal and soul-searching, but there was an album by Robert Fripp with that title already – in fact Phil had drummed on it!

"Then I wanted to call it *Interiors* because I wanted it to be an honest statement about me. But I couldn't call it that because Woody Allen had a film of the same name out at the same time."

(This affinity with comedians would later resurface with the second LP, *Hello, I Must Be Going!*, which is also the title of the Groucho Marx biography by Charlotte Chandler.)

Eventually he chose a title that was both obvious and perfect: *Face Value*.

When *Face Value* finally came out in February 1981, it wasn't released by Charisma (Genesis' label since 1970) because Phil had signed a new deal for his solo career.

"The reason I signed to Virgin was to get away from the nest. At this stage in my career, I found it best to make a clean break with Charisma, I had to get away from the bunch.

"I didn't want *Face Value* to be born with a noose around its neck, because so many people have connotations and preconceptions about Genesis. It would have been harmful for my record because it can appeal to the same people but it can also appeal to a lot more.

"I thought that anybody who would see an album by me out after I've been with Genesis for ten years and Brand X for five would think 'Oh, another Genesis album, thank you!' – whereas I think my album has great potential to appeal to more people than those who like Genesis.

"I deliberately went out of my way to change everything that people would automatically think about me, to try and bring the point home that I was something outside and very different from Genesis.

"The reason I went with Virgin was that I got a good feeling from the people I met . . . I didn't go round meeting lots of record companies, I just said I wanted somebody else and my manager Tony Smith went round and got the energy from different labels – I could have signed to CBS for a lot more money, but then I didn't want to be part of that. I liked the idea of going into a company and people knowing my name and me knowing their names.

"In America, I stayed with Atlantic because the same stigma with bands and labels doesn't apply there and also Ahmet Ertegun had given me a lot of encouragement and I didn't want to thank him by kicking him in the teeth! I like the people at Atlantic."

To most record-buyers, the change of record company may seem trivial – after all it's the music on the record that counts, not the label! But Phil is adamant that the move was necessary: "On Charisma it would have been just another solo album from the Genesis crowd. On Virgin, it's something different."

And so it was: not only had Collins written some great heartache, heartbreak ballads, but he'd created a hybrid of pop music and black rhythms – as graphically demonstrated by the presence on the same record of white blues guitarist Eric Clapton and the black funk of the Earth Wind & Fire brass section.

The music had a vital sixties feel, but with a contemporary setting. All that was required now was to get the product in the shops.

Even after the hours and hours cooped up in a studio recording all the ambient sounds and remixing the different frequencies, there's still another important stage before the album can be manufactured ready for shipping out to the record stores. Phil himself is certain that the way in which the lacquer cut (the technical operation that transfers the music from tape to vinyl) is performed can actually enhance the production work – if it's done right!

"In Genesis we'd never taken an incredible interest in the cut – it's only recently that I've discovered how important the cutting engineer is. He really has total control of something you've been spending months and thousands of pounds doing. You just go in and give him your master tape and he's like an extra producer – he can make it sound good or bad!"

Phil first flew to the US to cut *Face Value* at Sterling Sound in New York (which is mistakenly credited on the sleeve) but Phil wasn't convinced the sound was right, so he tried three different cuts at a mastering studio in London and still wasn't happy with the results.

"I wanted the record to sound very much like a black album. I think my music is different from a lot of people's music, simply because I'm taking black and white influences and creating something new."

In desperation, Phil went home to relax and to listen to some of his favourite music . . . Earth Wind & Fire and the Jacksons. "They sounded great, then I put on my acetate and . . . by comparison, it sounded tame."

Yet Phil was convinced he'd made a great record and all he needed was a good cut. So in the end: "I looked on the back of the sleeves of all these records I liked and the name Michael Reese kept coming up. 'Mastered by Michael Reese, The Mastering Lab, Los Angeles.'

"I thought 'shit, I'll just ring him up!' I got the number through Directory Enquiries and called him."

Because of pressure of work, Phil couldn't actually attend the cut, but gave Michael some basic instructions about levels on different tracks and let Reese do what he's best at. The results were exactly what Phil was hoping for.

"It was staggering. I put the cut on and it was *much* blacker, it just sounded better coming out of the speakers – the sound came out of the speaker as opposed to staying in it."

However, the story doesn't end there. It appears that two different versions of the album were eventually pressed up – the original Reese cut has TML stamped in the disc's run-off while the later "copy-cuts" (by Ian Cooper at the Townhouse) are stamped TOWNHOUSE on the rim. Some copies are reportedly even made up of one side cut by Reese and the other by Cooper!

When finally released in February 1981, the album received reviews that were ecstatic:

"The energy is succinct and the effect is highly charged. Phil's plaintive, naked vocals . . . from funky beat to melancholic ballads with occasional pop and avant garde twinges . . . Phil Collins wears plenty of hats. But he has never tried one that doesn't fit." – Hugh Fielder, SOUNDS.

Several people centred in on the fact that, apart from writing some great tunes (which was a huge surprise to virtually everyone!), Phil had also re-worked a Genesis song from *Duke*.

The album also featured one other cover version – the Beatle's swirling, psychedelic 'Tomorrow Never Knows' (from their 1966 *Revolver* album), which showed Collins' knack of recognising a good tune, even when it's a vastly underrated one. "I admired the Beatles because they had a sense of what was just right for the time."

By a macabre, ironic twist of fate, when Phil's first solo single, 'In the Air Tonight' was released, it was prevented from reaching Number One in Britain by John Lennon's savage murder and the following wave of public sympathy in which people rushed out to buy his old records as souvenirs of a great artist. And so, while 'In The Air Tonight' hovered at Number Three, the top two spots were occupied by 'Imagine' and 'Woman'. "I was upset when Lennon died," said Phil, "but I wasn't one of those people who went into mourning for two weeks. I found it unpleasant that the press and TV seemed to be getting everybody who knew Lennon to say their bit – including people that he had met briefly on a windy night in 1964.

"I thought the old Beatles producer George Martin summed Lennon's death up the best, when he said he was angry that such talent could have been destroyed in such a terrible way.

"Because I'm a musician, then Lennon's death obviously seems to be pretty close to home. He helped sculpt a whole generation and Beatles songs have become standards – perhaps there's no greater tribute to be made than people humming your songs."

But even Lennon's tragic death couldn't over-shadow the emergence of Phil Collins from out of the shadows into the spotlight. His first-ever solo single was a perfect choice: It had style, passion, identity – and a pounding rhythm.

"I'm gratified and a bit surprised that 'In The Air Tonight' is doing so well," he said at the time. "Even when you come from a well-known band, it's a gamble when you do things on your own. It was my favourite track on the album, but I thought the format was unconventional – particularly for DJs who like to have it delivered to them."

The appeal of the single was considerably enhanced by the accompanying promotional video which strikingly conveyed the stark emotional turmoil of the lyric by means of recreating the monochrome head shot from the album sleeve to show Phil singing the cutting lyrics in extreme close-up.

This was then intercut with a section (filmed in colour to suggest a dream sequence) of Phil leaving an empty, dingy room and wandering down an endless corridor opening door after door, searching, searching, searching . . .

It was a striking, low-key video which had a consider-able emotional impact on the viewer – a million miles away from the other glossy, pseudo-glamorous, escapist promo videos being made at the time by acts like Duran Duran and Spandau Ballet.

But the commercial success of the song as a hit single was due almost entirely to Atlantic boss Ahmet Ertegun who recognised the track as a potential hit single even when he first heard the rough demos, but suggested the off-beat was too dominant: "You'll get all the kids dancing to the wrong beat. You've got to spell it out a bit."

By the time Phil considered this advice fully, he had only just finished recording the album – "I couldn't bear the thought of going back to the studio and I told him.

"And he said 'All you've got to do is put a bit of drums on the song before the other drums come in. It's a hit if you do!'

"So I went back into the studio and did it. And he was right! I listened to it on the car radio the other day and I wouldn't have heard the beat properly if I hadn't put the extra drums on."

The success of both *Face Value* and especially 'In the Air Tonight' was followed by further Collins singles – 'I Missed Again' and 'If Leaving Me Is Easy' – but this in no way laid the path for a Genesis split. "Nobody ever thought Tony or Mike were leaving when they did their solo albums. Maybe I'm considered to be an outsider with the group.

"I guess I'm the clown of the line-up and a catalyst for the others. I don't fit into that neat public school mould that people are always putting Genesis in.

"Solo albums, if they're approached in the right context, don't mean the artist is bored with the band. They give him a chance to get things out of his system and build up his confidence as an individual.

"I know what people say about solo albums, but in our case, I can only say that doing them actually kept Mike and Tony in the band. The group is solid. But I can understand why bands split up. People grow up at different speeds and things get complicated.

"Doing this solo album, though, has been great for me – it's my very own music and I feel more complete for having recorded it."

8

AS EASY AS A, B, ABACAB

In the summer of 1981, Genesis came together for another artistic assault on their three-way alliance: they chose to retreat to the country to their own studio – The Farm in Surrey – to rehearse new material for their thirteenth album.

With a group like Genesis – with three song-writers who also record solo albums – you'd imagine there would be squabbles over whether new songs should be used for Genesis or kept back for solo recordings.

"Well I don't think it's like that," replies Phil. "I think it's a question of the fact that I like to play the keyboards on my things and obviously if you're in a band and you've got a keyboard player, he plays the keyboards! So, I don't really want to put my thing into the group with an individual song and say 'This is my song. How do you feel about playing it?' – I could get session musicians to do that!

"When I'm in the band, there's a group thinking, but outside the group I'm a free man. I'd like to spend less time on the road with Genesis . . . because I'd like to spend more time on the road with my own stuff."

Obviously Phil's recent success as a solo artist affected the schedule of work undertaken by Genesis, but it's an ironic truism of the entertainment world that the more famous and important entertainers become, the *less* work they do! When they're young, eager and struggling to make an impression, they're more than willing to play two shows a night and do anything else to achieve public acclaim. But once they've attained a certain level of fame, fortune and artistic respect, they can afford to pick and choose their appearances. Genesis are no different from other groups and it showed in their output – fewer tours, less promotional work and no new record for eighteen months.

Although this situation suited all three members of the band – and the leisurely break had allowed both Mike and Tony to record solo albums – Phil decided that he should now exert a degree of pressure on the other two to bring Genesis up to date in an attempt to shed their old 'pretentious/pompous' tag.

"I would love Genesis to get a different record label," he told journalists at the time. "If we moved to someone like Stiff, for example, that would be great. The music would be whatever we made but because the label would be different, people would approach it from a different angle. It would stop people short.

"I don't want to upset anybody at Charisma because I like everybody there and they do a fine job. Tony Stratton-Smith believed in us and people like Van Der Graaf Generator for years before people started taking notice – he has supported us all the way through. But perhaps we have to think of our own future."

And the future for Genesis in 1981 was a new album to be called *ABACAB*.

Apparently the name came from assigning the first three letters of the alphabet to three different sections of music that were later blended to create the title track.

"But when we finally put them together," adds Tony confusingly, "it spelt something completely different and unpronounceable!"

"A is Booker T and The MGs," begins Phil's explanation. "B is the Rolling Stones and C is 'Friday On My Mind' by the Easybeats. It's very much a group song – there are bits from everyone on that.

In fact, according to Phil: "*Duke* was very much a group album, but *ABACAB* was literally just us, especially as we produced it ourselves. We set out with the idea of writing a lot of songs together, and that's what we did.

"We spent fourteen weeks making *ABACAB*. If something wasn't happening, we'd stop and have a go at something else. Before, we'd have felt obliged to keep on trying to get it right."

Using their own studio, they didn't have to worry about running out of time or money and enabled the band to try every sort of permutation of each song: "There is a big difference" says Phil, "between working in our own studio and going away to do it and feeling you have to keep to a schedule."

Inspired by this new sense of freedom, they ended up with far more material than they needed. At one stage they even considered recording a double album, but – perhaps stung by the memory of *The Lamb Lies Down On Broadway* – decided against it.

Both Tony and Mike agreed that the group was developing a new sound, almost a radical new presentation of old values.

Tony: "This is the first album where the contributions are almost one third each. We tried to change our appeal slightly by altering the arrangements. We managed to change the character without necessarily changing the original composition that much.

"We just felt that we couldn't write any more songs about Greek myths – it was nice to streamline things and try to avoid some of our clichés, those things that had become almost second nature to us."

This was strikingly displayed by the use of brass on 'No Reply At All', an innovation suggested by Phil, who'd wanted to use the Earth Wind & Fire horns on *Duke* – "but I'd thought 'No way – black mafia and white boys? No chance!' Then I asked this guy at Atlantic Records in America to see what he could do and they agreed."

It seems that they'd heard some recent Genesis work and could see the direction in which the band were headed, and so immediately agreed to play on one track.

"So they arrived with their arranger Tom Tom. And he said 'Play the tape and sing into this cassette what you want to hear'. Next day they came in and played it."

Mike: "People tend to think of Genesis as a wall of sound, but I think that's a thing of the past."

This 'new' Genesis was certainly due in part to Phil Collins' recent confidence gained by his successful solo career. He gave Genesis a fresh outlook with a more direct approach – especially lyrically.

"I've always been a firm believer in the sound of the word, rather than what that word means. 'Follow You Follow Me' and 'Alone Tonight', for instance, are two songs of Mike's. In them he's trying to say 'I love you' – but the way he says 'I love you' is 'I love you, darling' as opposed to 'Shit, I miss you'. I really can't get behind those lyrics.

"I'm the singer of the group, I have to sing those lyrics. If someone's not the singer, they come in with lyrics that look good but aren't easy to sing. I've had all sorts of things to cope with – I mean, 'breadbin' was in one song, what the hell do you do with that?"

This sort of friendly criticism was in itself a sign that the three members of Genesis were willing to discuss freely the problems and attitudes of songwriting – when Phil first joined the group, people would regularly go for a long walk rather than talk to anyone about the music, simply because they felt so defensive and unsure about their own creativity.

But with Mike and Tony also having recorded their own solo records recently – and having sung on them too – they were more aware of the difficulties faced by a vocalist.

As Mike explained: "When I write stuff for Phil to sing, I often write things that sound good in my head, but when you try to actually sing them, they turn out not to be good vocal phrases. But I know that now . . ."

And so *ABACAB* saw another shift in the band's songwriting stance towards shorter, sharp melodic pop songs, featuring ten songs in all; one solo composition each and seven group collaborations. With the emphasis now on sounds rather than rambling tales of mythical characters, this LP continued the trend set by *Duke* of not featuring a lyric sheet.

Perhaps fans might have been surprised that now Phil

had established himself as a songwriter of international fame, that he didn't dominate writing credits. But that was the last thing on his mind.

"With Genesis I've got into a certain style of writing lyrics because we all spread the writing of lyrics amongst ourselves, unless someone's written the whole song themselves, but nowadays that won't happen.

"I'm not interested in putting my own songs into Genesis – I'd rather keep them for myself and submit little bits and pieces that the band can expand upon.

ABACAB was finally released in September 1981; the reviewers immediately picked up on the album's brand of spontaneous energy, as Cathi Wheatley in Sounds advised potential buyers that "No-one is to be lulled into a false sense of security on this album. The title track is probably one of the best things that Genesis have ever done – raunchy, lively stuff showing Collins at his most streetwise and all three at their most innovative."

Indeed the title track (as well as 'No Reply At All') became a smash hit in America *and* Britain, which gave Genesis a completely new audience but still didn't really change their public image of being aloof and pretentious art-rockers.

"The hit singles have just turned our hard-core fans against us!" complained Phil at the time. "They say that we've sold out. But they don't really understand the group either, in that case.

"There's a certain type of fan – in the old days it used to be the trench coat and the fishing hat with the albums under their arms . . . but they're the guys, even though they're caricatures of themselves, that did help us carry on doing what we wanted to do.

"Let's face it, if the band doesn't sell records, then you can't carry on. But all we have ever been, is a group that writes songs. We've never stood for anything in particular, we've just written songs and the songs are sometimes three minutes and sometimes ten minutes and sometimes twenty-five minutes long, but they're SONGS with melodic content and lyrics that aren't just 'baby, baby, baby' which is what Robert Plant does so well.

"So, they don't seem to understand that if we put out a three-minute song like 'Follow You, Follow Me', it's because that song wouldn't sound any good ten minutes long. It's a concise piece of music at three minutes long and to us, it's just as important or relevant as something like 'Supper's Ready'."

Tony Banks is quick to second this view. "We'd put out maybe fifteen or twenty singles which didn't sell any before we had a hit with 'Follow You, Follow Me'," he adds. "We just carried on releasing them and suddenly the radio started playing them so we said 'Thanks very much!'."

But still the spectre of Genesis' beginnings and the legacy of Gabriel's theatrical image hung like a mill-stone around their neck. It was a problem of which all the band were aware, none more so than Collins.

When this author suggested to him that comparisons with such rock dinosaurs as Yes, ELO, Moody Blues and Pink Floyd were partly justified, Phil Collins conceded that it might have been true once, but simply because "that's the period we happened to come up in.

"Now, I personally don't like any of those groups," he explained with some patience, "so it angers and frustrates me when we get compared to them, because I think we have a lot more substance and a lot more balls and we're constantly questioning ourselves much more than any of that lot.

"We've tried to change our music over the years, we've *tried* and we have developed because we keep our ears to the ground a bit more than maybe someone like the Moody Blues. I know that we've done some things that could be termed 'pompous' – but that was then! There are certain elements of Genesis that I still don't like.

"But like everybody else, we look and dress and think differently from the way we did five years ago. And as far as I'm concerned, we sound different too."

And the difference wasn't solely down to the new influence of Phil Collins, solo performer, although his impact was still enormous.

For years he had sat behind the drums, content to

merely suggest a line here and a snatch of melody there, but he'd never really been a positive force in the scheme of Genesis songwriting.

"In fact," he admits candidly, "I had never finished writing a song for the group before 'Misunderstanding', which was our first big hit in America. Suddenly my solo album came out and I was seen as a bit of a writer and my opinion in the group was given a bit more weight, which Tony and Mike appreciated, I think.

"I was there to say 'How about this here and how about that there?'. Maybe I made it more palatable, maybe I took it away from those self-conscious, grandiose settings by putting a bit of funk rhythm into it.

"As far as writing goes, we're all on an equal footing now. We seem to have much more common ground between us."

This was confirmed by Tony Banks who commented, "The band has always been a democracy, more so now perhaps than ever. Immediately after Steve Hackett left, Mike and I dominated the band for an album or two, but Phil is an equal partner now."

Returning the compliment, Phil says: "Tony's got his ear much more to the ground and his music's changing. We're now writing modern music and we're being influenced by bands that people don't even think we like."

In particular, Collins' own roots of black R'n'B and pop went much further than merely having the Earth Wind & Fire horn section guesting on certain songs – his love for pop simplicity gave the Genesis tradition for overblown epic anthems a new directness and brevity.

In return, ex-public schoolboys Rutherford and Banks added a degree of warmth and sophistication to Phil's tendency to create songs of almost embarrassingly naked minimalism.

"We've found with the last couple of albums with Genesis, that the most stimulating stuff for us has been when we've sparked off ideas by someone bringing a little bit of music into the room that they can't develop on their own," says Phil, "and someone else has picked it up and made something out of it – and suddenly there's a group song: it's a true combination, the chemistry between three people. And because it's a group, it's something we can't do individually."

With each of them also recording their own solo albums, Genesis managed to avoid most of the unsightly squabbles over songwriting that had marred the last couple of Beatles LPs.

And because they were all happy with the collaborative group songs, nobody felt resentful that anyone else should hold back solo songs for their own projects. As Phil reasoned when talking of Tony's own LP: "All the songs he's written himself . . . it saves me playing on his stuff and he doesn't have to play on my stuff!"

The success of the singles was highlighted by a new Genesis tour of Europe throughout the Autumn of 1981, culminating with four nights at Birmingham's cavernous National Exhibition Centre for which there were over three-quarters of a million ticket applications.

But the same year, Genesis had made a positive move to overcome the attendant problems of large concert halls where it's difficult to communicate with the audience – they played a few gigs at the Marquee, with a capacity crowd of just 500!

"We just thought it was a nice idea," explained Phil. "We'd never done it and we thought it would be fun to go back and do a one-off gig.

As had been proved by the choice of title for their 1978 album, *And Then There Were Three*, their self-deprecating sense of humour had lessened their tendency towards the pompous and bombastic elements of their music.

"There's a lot of humour that goes over everyone's heads" complains Phil with a sigh of resignation befitting a misunderstood artist.

Of course, any group that regularly dreams up titles such as 'Squonk', 'Wot Gorilla?' and 'Dodo' could hardly be accused of taking themselves too solemnly. But giving their fans value for money is a much more serious matter, which is why Genesis decided to revive the ancient noble custom of extended-play singles . . . and so, in May 1982, Charisma Records released '3 × 3' featuring three previously-unreleased tracks recorded during the *ABACAB* sessions.

"EPs are basically a forgotten art," says Phil. "We kept being told in America we couldn't release an EP – yet EPs used to be part of the rock'n'roll institution.

"So when we released the '3 × 3' EP, we did a Beatles parody: we thought we'd have a nice EP cover, we'll all jump off a wall in black-and-white and we'll have the same typeface . . . everything, so if you put the 'Twist And Shout' EP next to our EP, there's no difference except our faces."

To make the parody as perfect as possible, they even asked publicist Tony Barrow to recreate the same style of sleeve-notes as he had done for The Beatles almost twenty years earlier! "We said to him 'Go over the top' and he loved it!"

Unfortunately, not everyone shared Barrow's enthusiasm – the singles reviewer at NME probably wasn't even born when The Beatles' original EP was released, so he attacked the Genesis parody sleeve as though it were sincere and pompous! "And the humour went completely above his head," says Phil in mock disbelief. Luckily the general public didn't share this sense of uninformed cynicism and the EP reached Number Eight in the UK singles chart.

Gradually increasing numbers of music fans were beginning to realise that Genesis were becoming much more accessible.

"I think generally people would like us much more at a gig than on an album," reckons Phil, "because that's where our humour becomes apparent – obviously there's something to look at. And I try to deflate any kind of overblown pompousness that we've had, or appear to have.

"See, I've had this theory, ever since I started doing the singing with Genesis, that if you make people laugh, they relax.

"And if they're relaxed, they absorb more. They come off the edge of their seat, but unfortunately, I think with Genesis especially, people tend to take us far too seriously."

Tony Banks finds it difficult to appreciate why the band received such a 'serious' reputation in the first place. "I always saw us as having more to do with melodrama than anything else, and melodrama by its nature is not too serious – it's always got that tongue-in-cheek element."

But sometimes the dividing line between parody and truth gets a little blurred, as Phil discovered to his cost.

"On one Genesis tour I remember I was definitely drinking too much. I was drinking a lot around that time anyway, but we did a song called 'Say It's Alright Joe', which involved me dressing up as a Tony Hancock-type character and having a drink on stage.

"Of course, I had to have the real thing, so I was drinking an entire bottle of scotch a night. That song used to wreck the entire set for me."

A further sell-out US tour was followed by a third live album, the double-record set *Three Sides Live* in June 1982.

This rather confusing title derived from the fact that only the UK edition of the record actually featured four sides of live recordings!

Elsewhere, *Three Sides Live* was just that – sides one, two and three were exactly the same as the UK album, but the three live songs from side four were replaced by the '3 × 3' EP tracks, which had never previously been released in America.

It was also a rather neat pun in the Genesis tradition: this was, after all, live LP number three for the band, just as the live set *Seconds Out* had been their second!

The tracks on *Three Sides Live* blended together different versions by different Genesis line-ups, thus including appearances by Steve Hackett and Bill Bruford as well as Chester Thompson and Daryl Stuermer in what was described by Sounds as "an updated Greatest Hits package".

To coincide with this live album, Genesis returned to Italy in August 1982 to tour the country which had first rewarded them with audience acclaim and loyalty.

There was an unexpected reunion between Genesis and Peter Gabriel in October when they played a special benefit gig in the rain at Milton Keynes Bowl in aid of the

WOMAD festival (an ambitious multi-ethnic cultural event that Gabriel had helped organise but which was a financial disaster despite being an artistic triumph).

It was a suprise event for which Genesis had insisted on not being mentioned in any advance publicity, even though they opened the show. Peter Gabriel was then carried onstage in a coffin by four undertakers for he and the band to combine forces for old selections like 'Music Box' and 'Supper's Ready', while the band tried to back Peter on an unrehearsed version of his solo hit 'Solsbury Hill'.

The whole show climaxed when Steve Hackett joined them on stage for the encore of 'I Know What I Like' (featuring a rather shaky duet between Peter and Phil) and 'The Knife' – which, according to Hugh Fielder in Sounds, "set the perfect seal on the evening and by then it didn't matter what they sounded like".

It was the perfect close to a year which had witnessed Genesis flexing their collective artistic muscle and proving without doubt that they weren't yet ready for retirement!

9

PRODUCTION WORK

Phil Collins was by now a hugely popular man – in more ways than one. His solo success had not only brought him fame and fortune while causing even cynical critics to view Genesis in a new light, but he'd also become a most respected producer among his fellow musicians.

Of course, he'd always been in demand for his drumming ability on recording sessions ever since 1971, when he'd worked on an album with singer Colin Scot which was cosily entitled *Colin Scot And Friends!*

From then on, there was no stopping him, and whenever he had spare time from the Genesis schedule, he'd always prefer to take his drums into a studio session than lie on a beach getting tanned.

During the ten years between 1971 and 1981, Phil appeared on numerous records by top class artists, including Argent, John Cale, Thin Lizzy, Café Jacques, Robert Fripp, John Martyn and Brian Eno as well as contributing percussion to several film soundtracks including 'Operation Daybreak' (1975) – featuring Timothy Bottoms and Martin Shaw – and 'The Squeeze' (1977) starring Stacy Keach, Edward Fox and David Hemmings.

In addition, he'd also worked closely with various other musicians close to the Genesis camp, appearing on solo albums by ex-members Peter Gabriel and Steve Hackett as well as an instrumental album released by Ringo Starr's label Ring O'Records called *Startling Music* which was recorded by David Hentschel, who was best known for his work with Genesis in various capacities – engineer on *A Trick Of The Tail*, co-producer on *Wind And Wuthering, Seconds Out, And Then There Were Three* and *Duke*, and even as a backing vocalist on *Duke*!

But, on a more permanent note, Phil had increasingly spent his spare time away from Genesis simply playing for fun with his 'other' group, Brand X.

Since coming together for some sessions at Island Studios – which resulted in the *The Eddie Howell Gramophone Record* – guitarist John Goodsall, bassist Percy Jones, keyboardist Robin Lumley and Collins as drummer had collectively recorded seven albums. However, they regarded themselves as a fluid aggregate of like-minded musicians inspired by free-form jazz and funk rather than a steady group with a line-up confined to just four people.

"It's good music and good fun to play. But I hate that phrase jazz-funk, it's so crass! Although our tunes with Brand X are structured in a very loose way," Phil told Melody Maker, "I think we'd all like to have even more relaxation on stage, more blowing . . ."

This open attitude meant that guest musicians were always welcome at Brand X sessions: in fact, because of Phil's other commitments (notably with Genesis), they were often essential! During the second half of 1978, for instance, he was committed to a Genesis world tour, which meant he was unable to be involved with the fourth Brand X LP, *Masques*, on which his place on drums was taken by Chuck Burgi.

However, by the time Phil's marriage had broken up, he realised that he was probably over-working and that he should concentrate any spare energy and creativity on his solo career, which allowed him to indulge his own taste and influences to the full.

After five years of occasional small tours and large recording sessions, Brand X ground to a halt and the final testament to their free-wheeling attitude appeared in September 1982 when Robin Lumley remixed the tapes of surplus material from earlier studio sessions to produce *Is There Anything About?* their seventh album.

The reviews were particularly cruel, which riled Phil out

of his normally placid nonchalance.

"Did you read the review?" he enquired of this author the following week. "It was ridiculous: 'New album from Brand X, fusion-jazz' which is all in the past, I don't play that any more, I'm not a jazz buff, I'm not really into that area of jazz like Art Ensemble etc – it reminds me of what Phil Seamen once said: 'Avant garde is great to play but painful to listen to'."

"Then it continued: 'from Genesis drumboid Phil Collins and doesn't he like us to know it.' I thought 'What's all this about?'."

The review in Sounds went on to describe the music as "jazz-rock flatulence" and Brand X as "a crack team of deathly dull musician-types who insist on boring the listener by cranking out the kind of laid-back easy on the ear, late-night anthems that are the probable cause of motorway pile-ups."

In fact, Brand X's seventh and final album, *Is There Anything About?* was released by CBS Records without Phil's knowledge.

"I had nothing to do with this album . . . I played on it two or three years ago and then Robin Lumley, the keyboard player, took the tapes and bolstered them up, but I guess because I'm the most famous guy in the band, it's my band!

"One of the reasons I stopped playing with Brand X was that too many people thought it was my thing. And I didn't like all of it enough to say 'This is my thing'."

And so Phil simply stopped his association with Brand X, but swiftly began working with a diverse cross-section of respected musicians, ranging from female vocalists to funk brass sections.

But of all the artists and groups with whom he worked, Phil found the most inspirational to be Brian Eno, *enfant terrible* of avant-garde pop and ex-keyboard player with Roxy Music. So what did Phil learn from working with Eno on two albums, *Another Green World* and *Before And After Science*?

"It's the spirit," he replies immediately. "I liked his idea of just getting people together and working off the top of your head. It's the attitude – 'I don't really know what I'm doing, I'm not really a musician, but let's have a bit of fun anyway'. I thought that was great and I still do.

"I remember a classic; Eno gave us all a bit of paper and we made lists from one to fifteen. Eno said 'Number two, we all play a G, number seven we all play a C sharp' and so on.

"So it was like painting by numbers. And it's that kind of bravery – he was prepared to waste an awful lot of time and money just to find out what it sounded like. He used to love me and Percy Jones (the bassist from Brand X) – we would go in and run through our dictionary of licks and he'd record them and make a tape loop of them."

Phil had high hopes that his excellent work on those two albums might be his passport to playing with David Bowie. "The sun suddenly shone out of Eno's arse, and the putting together of what he did, with the hip rhythms and stuff – that was me and Percy. I was hoping to get a call from Bowie because he had then got Eno to produce his album. I never did though . . ."

But Phil's obvious disappointment at not getting to work with Bowie was cushioned by the respect he was earning from other contemporary artists. And soon he was being regarded as a record producer of quality, other artists were asking him to take complete charge of their albums in an effort to gain the magical touch that had made 'In The Air Tonight' such an international smash.

"The first thing I produced was my own album, *Face Value*. After that, John Martyn asked me to produce his album, *Glorious Fool*, because we were mates. I love John Martyn, we're very close – but that was the first time I'd been asked to produce anybody. I was a bit scared, but we did it and it turned out pretty well . . . in fact, it did better than any previous album he'd done."

Collins had already played on John Martyn's 1980 album, *Grace And Danger*, and had even been part of Martyn's backing band that did a short tour in 1981. There's a close affinity between the two men and Phil is naturally stung by criticism that he shouldn't have worked with Martyn in the first place.

"A lot of people who have cast shadows over what I do, think John was doing all right until he met me and then I fucked him up by putting him in a group! In fact, *he* wanted to work with a group because he'd done it all on his own and it was just coincidence that I was working with him! "He's got a wonderful voice and he writes great songs and I'm a huge fan of his. In fact, the reason I originally did *Glorious Fool* is because I didn't want anyone else to mess it up!

"I was a friend of his and I said 'Look, if I do it, at least I'll know that nobody else will ruin it!' "

As a producer, Collins was still learning by experience and playing it by ear, almost literally.

"I like what I hear, or I don't like what I hear" is how he sums up his own talent as a producer. "Like the title of George Martin's book says – 'All You Need Is Ears'. That's what it all comes down to. George Martin, like Quincy Jones and Phil Spector, is a great producer . . . but I would never call myself a producer in those terms. Really, I'm just someone who directs a song into a certain area – and I know what I like to hear when I put a record on."

But really, Phil is much more than just a producer or a director – he's a session drummer, a fellow-musician, a confidante, songwriter, singer and all-round motivator in the studio.

"When I work with somebody, I like to get totally involved in their project. I think a lot of people want my distinctive drum sound. They believe that if they get me, they get the drum sound. But I want to make it as much a part of me as it is a part of them."

This was certainly the case with ex-Abba vocalist, Frida. She and Phil seemed inevitably drawn together by fate and their mutual sadness.

"We've both been through broken relationships" she explained at the time. "I think that's why I knew we would work together so well. I listened to a lot of Phil's work because my daughter likes it, and I found that we were totally in tune with each other."

But what made Phil want to work with Frida?

"The way I heard it was that there were a couple of

people around who wanted me to produce their album, but Frida – for some reason – became the most important. Important being because, I thought 'Abba, y'know, very successful group known for their pop records and everyone says they've got classic production – and here's one of them wants me to produce her album. This has gotta be worth looking into.'

"The reason she wanted me to do it was because she had been through her own situation and I guess I'm getting a tag for being a producer who only works with people who have been divorced – John Martyn was the first, then Frida . . . it seems to be a foregone conclusion that I won't work with anyone else!

"I like to think she felt I'd be sympathetic, that if – being a lady – she didn't want to come in after a particularly hard night emotionally, I would be sympathetic rather than saying 'Hey, what is this? Come in and work!'."

Because of the Abba reputation – not to mention Frida's brilliant voice – this was one challenge Phil couldn't turn down and so he travelled to Polar Studios in Stockholm where he became totally involved in the project from first to last: choosing the material, playing the drums on the backing tracks, producing the overall sound with engineer Hugh Padgham and eventually mixing the final versions – seven weeks in all.

This album was his first stab at what he terms 'real' production – "for the first time I had people looking over my shoulder about budgets; I had to book the musicians – it was a much more serious project. Although there's a lot of money in that organisation, it was still a budget-conscious album.

"I mean, Abba . . . they're worth a fortune. Just saying they're as big as Volvo is too easy – their turnover is 200 million Kroner a year without the music, that's just their investments!"

This was graphically illustrated by a classic incident when Phil and Hugh had a day off from studio and decided to go for a sauna.

"So we asked Frida where we could go and she said there was a really nice old building in the centre of

Stockholm which had got steambaths.

"And we said 'But we're not members' and she said 'That's OK – I own it!'."

But recording the album was much more serious business. Because Frida didn't write her own songs, the initial task for Phil was to sit down with her and choose the material. "We had tapes coming out of our ears! There was no shortage of songs . . . but there really weren't that many good songs, or songs that I liked anyway!

"We had Squeeze submitting songs, Elvis Costello submitting songs – I only heard two of the three songs he submitted, but I didn't think they were very good! And I didn't think they were good for Frida.

"I mean, I like Elvis and some of the songs he writes are fantastic, though I prefer his earlier stuff compared with his later stuff. So it wasn't like it was a classic song that I didn't want to use – and anyway, if Frida had liked it, I'd have given it a second chance.

"There was a Joe Jackson song I was quite keen on but Frida wasn't sure and the Squeeze song was a very British song – you can't get Frida singing a song about life in Clapham! It's got nothing to do with her! There were certain things that were right and certain things that were wrong.

"Stephen Bishop writes great songs and so I said 'Have you got any songs for her?' and there is one which is the title of his new album, 'Sleeping With Girls', which would have been fantastic, but he wouldn't let me have it!

"Plus there were a couple of songs that Frida chose from Sweden, which are not my favourite songs . . ."

It was a strange partnership for both artists. For Frida, it was a bewildering change to be given such a degree of freedom and responsibility after the successful but claustrophobic, rigid discipline of the Abba hit-machine.

"In the Abba set-up" explained Phil, "poor old Agnetha and Frida were never asked questions, they were told 'Sing this! Yes, that's great! Thank you!' So for someone like me to come and say to Frida 'What key do you want this in? Do you want it rocky or is this too fast for you?' – the first week she was 'I don't know, what do *you* think?', but I said 'Listen, it's your album baby, it's not mine'. And after two or three weeks, she really started to come through."

Aided by engineer Hugh Padgham, Phil worked on presenting Frida's classic voice in an updated rock setting: "I tended to go for the sound that each particular song should sound like. There are many songs on the Frida album that sound very different."

It seemed that Frida was looking to establish herself as a contemporary rock performer rather than as a female singer in the style of, say, Barbra Streisand or Diana Ross.

As Phil explains, "She was looking at Pat Benatar, Kim Wilde who haven't even got as good a voice – Frida has got a fantastic voice, she opens her mouth and she sings perfectly – she saw all this happening around her and she wanted to get into it."

Although the collaboration of Phil and Frida was only partially successful, certain tracks at least showed just what she was capable of as a vocalist, notably the classic pop of 'I Know There's Something Going On' – with its instantly recognisable Phil Collins drum pattern – which became a hit in several countries and gave the album its title of *Something's Going On.*

As Phil says, "If you're a singer and you don't write songs, then Russ Ballard is exactlly the sort of person you look to!" Ballard already had an impressive track record, both as a songwriter for other artists (including hits for Argent, Barry Ryan and Leo Sayer) and as a solo singer, but it was the Collins production and the Collins drum sound that made it so distinctive.

Despite that undoubted highlight, the Frida album was decidedly patchy. Several tracks were simply not convincing songs, while a couple of others lacked conviction in the delivery – especially 'Here We'll Stay' which was a tortured duet between Frida and Phil!

"Well . . . that was a complete lapse of taste on my part! I think it's hideous too!" he admits sheepishly. "This is one thing I'm not gonna try and get out of. I said to Frida 'I don't mind singing on the album' – now, in fact, the backing track to that song stood up much better than the actual finished article. The reason we chose the song was that it was a great song for the horns and a great song for us to play as a band.

"When we chose the song, Frida said 'Maybe you could sing this too', because I was singing it to her to try and get her to loosen up a bit. I mean, if you're from a foreign country and you try to sing English lyrics, there's a borderline between sounding convincing and not sounding convincing. And I didn't think she was sounding very convincing . . .

"But you've gotta draw it out of someone, you can't just expect someone – even if they're from one of the most successful groups in the world – to just come out and do it.

"So we were drawing it out and some of her vocal performances were very good. But . . . she said 'Maybe you could sing this with me' and I didn't at the time actually think of it as a duet. I just thought 'Yeah, OK, maybe we could both sing all of it', like a combination of voices.

"But then it became apparent that the key of the song was too low for her – which meant that I had to sing some of it – but it was too high for me, so she had to sing some of it too . . . and it ended up sounding like Rita Coolidge and Kris Kristofferson!

"I was committed to it by this point, so I put blinkers on and went down the whole way mixing it – and then of course, they tried to put it out as a single, and I said 'No way! I don't wanna be associated with this as a single'.

"We used the record company excuse that Atlantic, Virgin and Charisma would cause a fuss because it was my voice, but . . . ah, never again!"

While he obviously has some regrets about that one song, he looks back fondly on the album as a whole.

"I enjoyed doing it, because it was great for me to have responsibility for all the production – it was the first proper production I'd done in terms of being in charge of the budget *and* the songs.

"And now I know that I can do it, you know, holding all the production reins – dealing with people and with money . . . I was very pleased with the way it turned out. I viewed it as a great challenge and had a great time.

"But her next album will be much better."

Frida, for one, had no doubts about the merits of the album.

"Phil's such a good producer, and a very nice guy. I'm sure I couldn't have done it without him and we've made plans to work together again sometime soon."

Unfortunately, pressure of work meant that Phil was already committed to other projects though he'd earlier said he'd be more than happy to work with Frida again – "If I don't it will be purely because I've already done that and I want to do something else."

10

HELLO, I MUST BE GOING

"Although I had no material written, I really wanted to make another album. So I gave myself five weeks: I came back from doing Frida's album on the Friday, sat down at the piano on the Monday and started writing songs at home. Some of it was good, some of it was crap."

To being with, it was hard work. After all, he'd set an incredibly high standard with *Face Value*, and having spent several months away from home producing Frida's album, Phil was in no frame of mind to simply turn on his creative talent and come up with a new clutch of instant classics.

"Well, I don't actually sit down and say 'I'm going to write today' – I'm not prolific in that way. I can't actually turn it on . . . what I do is doodle around the piano and if something comes up and I like it, I'll use it! If something comes up that I've heard before, then I won't and if something comes up that *I've* done before, I won't – it won't go any farther than that. So, my better lyrics are lyrics pertaining to me."

But Phil's second album – which he called *Hello, I Must Be Going* after the hilarious Groucho Marx biography by Charlotte Chandler – still betrayed many confused emotions, as shown even by the song titles alone.

On one hand there was the continuing sadness and despair of 'I Cannot Believe It's True' and 'Don't Let Him Steal Your Heart Away', but these were counterbalanced by a new self-confidence (admittedly laced with severe bitterness) as portrayed by 'I Don't Care' and 'It Don't Matter To Me'.

"The main difference between this album and *Face Value* was that this time I didn't have the impetus of the divorce and the emotional upheaval I'd had before.

"But if you're unhappy, you tend to write very melancholy stuff and it worked last time. There is no doubt that *Face Value* was the result of feeling miserable – it wasn't meant as a useful dictionary for people who are getting divorced. I just happened to be on the receiving end of that situation and I spent my time writing. I was incredibly low and playing such mournful chords on the piano; quite revelling in my depression.

"It's like a different situation now and . . . I don't *only* write love songs and I don't want to have this image of being someone that middle-aged contented couples come and see for singalongaPhil . . . even though I'm a very romantic person.

'I'm sure there's a harder edge to me than that, so this new LP's more 'UP'. It's funny because I thought I only had one album in me. But the second album wasn't as hard as I thought it would be, because after the sorrow comes the bitterness. There are songs that relate to the divorce period but rather than 'Why are you gone?' it's more a case of 'You're gone and I'm getting up . . .' "

Having finished off a complete set of nine new songs, Phil laid down backing tracks at the Farm studio – where he decided to do a new version of the Supremes 'You Can't Hurry Love' – and then added some overdubs and finished the album off at the Townhouse in London.

Musically, *Hello, I Must Be Going* had a fuller, less sparse sound, to reflect its happier mood. Gone was the Roland rhythm box which had given *Face Value* such a homemade feel and, in its place, half of the tracks featured either a string section arranged by Martyn Ford or the Phenix Horns, and featuring the world premiere of Phil himself as a trumpeter on 'Do You Know, Do You Care?'

Lyrically, as Phil had already said, his songs were less directly concerned with dark yesterdays and concentrated instead on brighter tomorrows.

This was best demonstrated by the opening track, 'I Don't Care Any More', which was full of quietly confident defiance as expressed by the following verses:

'You can tell everybody about the state I'm in,
You won't catch me crying, cause I just can't win,
I don't care any more.

Well I don't care now what you say,
Cause every day I'm feeling fine with myself,
And I don't care now what you say,
I'll do all right by myself.'

However, a track like the moving 'Don't Let Him Steal Your Heart Away' brought back all the old anguish and desolation with a pleading tone that bordered on despair.

'Don't pack my suitcase, I'll be back,
Don't take my pictures off of the wall,
Don't let him change a thing, cause I'll be back,
Just tell him to pack his things and get out of your life,
Just give me one more chance, I'll show you I'm right.'

Right: Flaming Youth – young Phil is in the foreground
Below: Genesis 1973

Left: Genesis today – with Chester and Daryl
Below left: Peter Gabriel in all his glory
Below centre: ''He went thataway . . .''
Below right: Young at heart

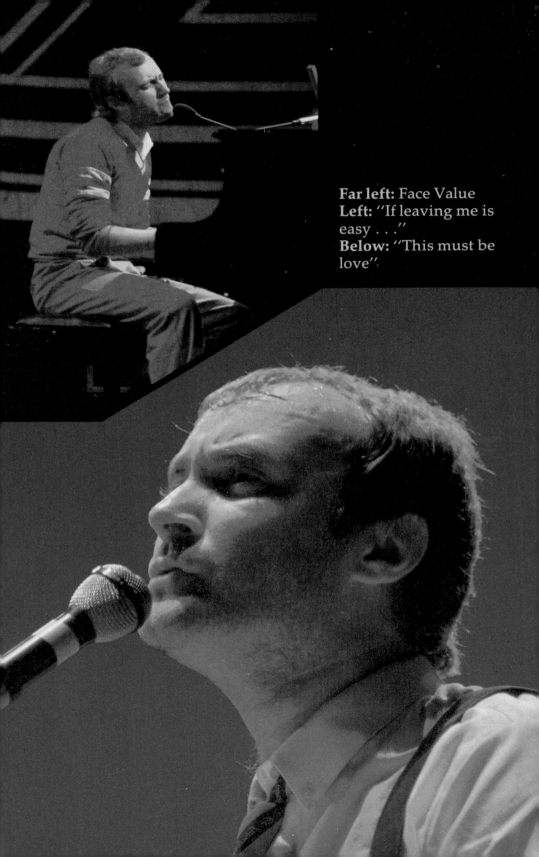

Far left: Face Value
Left: "If leaving me is easy . . ."
Below: "This must be love".

Left: "Hang on, I've got the words in my pocket . . ."
Right: Phil with two of his admirers!
Below: Phil with his wife, Jill

Inset: Live Aid — the
global jukebox!
From London to
Philadelphia

Main pic: At
Wembley with Sting

Deliberately, Phil chose to show the public a happier, almost exuberant public face compared to his previous image, and so the first single to be taken from the album was the up-tempo 'You Can't Hurry Love'.

This was promoted by an hilarious video, showing three different versions of Phil on split screens merged to look like one scene depicting a vocal trio.

It was a very simple idea brilliantly executed – even if there *are* a couple of instances where Phil number two seems to materialise through a microphone stand! – where the element of irrepressible humour doesn't detract from the basic energy of the performance.

"The video was just meant to be a replica of the song," explains Phil. "I wanted it to be like those old, really bad promotional videos where everyone's jacket was too small and trousers too short by couple of inches. And we had three of me on the video – just like The Supremes!"

Both video and single became an instant success and acted as tasters for the album: quite an irony for a sixties cover version to herald the release of a record full of original songs inspired by that very Motown sound.

When this author interviewed Phil at the time of his second album, he asked whether there was ever the temptation to throw in little snatches of lyric or melody into his own songs to pay homage to Tamla Motown or early R'n'B songs?

"No, but Little Steven – Miami Steve Van Zandt – there's a lot of Motown on his album, there's literally almost a parody of 'Tears Of A Clown' on that album.

"Actually I do it more with the Beatles – I mean, I was looking for a few middle eights for some of the songs on my new album and I found them, just by the kind of chords they used to use. They're not too hard to find if you look for them – but that to me is my history; The Beatles first with Motown, Stax and Atlantic very, very close seconds."

In fact, to acknowledge this, he had already recorded 'Tomorrow Never Knows' for *Face Value* and on the inner sleeve of the *Hello, I Must Be Going*, he wrote, "Motown we salute you!"

And as with those great sixties classics, most of Phil's material dealt with love, mainly of the broken-hearted variety.

"I'm very proud of things like 'If Leaving Me Is Easy', that hits right on the button how one feels in that situation.

"It's funny . . . on one hand, if I'm not unhappy, then people will think the unhappy songs I write are not genuine. But really it's all coming from the things that have happened to me and relating to that experience. I don't want to flush it out. Obviously there are certain ghosts that you want to exorcise, which have gone already. But it's part of your life, you can't just blot it out."

Some people were still surprised that a member of Genesis – a band still regarded as writing mostly about mythology and fables – could create such harrowing and honest songs.

"I prefer being on my own," says Phil by way of clarification, "because it means I can be more personal. I'm not a public schoolboy, but the rest of Genesis are. And when I was just writing for them, I was just writing stories all the time. Now I can write personally, the songs are what I feel."

But surely not all Phil's solo compositions are written from personal experience – what about 'Through These Walls', which is about a voyeur?

"Well that one wasn't!" he laughs "But . . . I like to watch, y'know. I'm a fan of watching. At the same time, I don't sit up at a wall with a glass . . . because I've no neighbours, y'see!

"For that video, I played a voyeur – a sort of dirty old young man! I had a dressing-gown, glass to listen at the wall and women's lingerie – three essential items for the successful pervert.

"I don't know why I always go for these seedy characters but it's all very lightweight. 'Through These Walls' just came from a line I heard somewhere else: 'I can hear through these walls'."

However, although Phil is no voyeur, he *is* an observer and he does have that vital ability to dramatise his

observations of everyday events for the purposes of songwriting.

"Because I like to watch," he explains, "I can use that as a tool to write lyrics – for instance, 'Like China' is basically a flippant song, a fun song; it's a story rather than a personal song and it's about the nights I'm sure everybody's experienced – you're fifteen or sixteen and your mum and dad have gone out and you've got your girlfriend round and you spend most of the evening trying to convince her that the best thing she can possibly do is to make love to you on the sofa.

"The song has the guy being a little aggressive, because that's what you're like when you're a teenager. Really, he's a bit hurt that this girl won't take her dress off!"

There was some criticism though, that as a creative statement, the *Hello, I Must Be Going* album was merely a pale retread of the intensely personal *Face Value*. Paul Colbert's review in Melody Maker mentioned 'now predictable moments' and decided that 'contentment has softened his focus and drawn the teeth that gave *Face Value* its bite.'

Phil flatly denies this. "No, I don't think that. I had a distinct lack of judgement on 'Through These Walls' when I used the same drum fill as 'In The Air Tonight', but to me that's where the comparison ends.

"Paul Colbert from Melody Maker wrote that bad review of my album and said it was a retread of the first album and I said to him 'I can tell you from my heart, it wasn't! I deliberately avoided anything that would be possible comparisons because people are going to compare it because they've only had one other album from me' – so why should I lay my neck on the line?

"I did everything in my power to stop those comparisons, so I didn't do certain things and I tried to bring more guitar in to make it different. And he sort of said 'well, yeah, I see . . .' – and he believed me because I'd told him from my heart."

Of course, comparisons between the two albums are inevitable simply because they are both the creation of the same artist. As Phil says, "It's my voice and I'm writing

about the same sorts of emotions. I still pull on that area two years ago. Although it was a depressing time, I got stimulated by it – it was great to be depressed!''

But bad reviews aren't news to Phil.

''I think apart from Hugh Fielder at Sounds, who I like as a bloke and we get on very well, I can't think of any journalist who actually likes Genesis!

''If I know that a journalist is in the audience and he doesn't like us, I'll still be more interested in him than in the 19,999 fans who do like us because I'm convinced that maybe he's barking up the wrong tree.''

Do you read the press avidly?

''Oh yes. Jill buys all the music papers every week. Some people say 'Why read them? If you get upset by them, don't read them!' But if I didn't read them, I'd probably figure they were saying far worse things than they actually are when I read them!''

In fact, in November 1982, the actuality of what the press were writing about Phil became much more vilifying than he could ever imagine, and this prompted him to write a series of letters to the Melody Maker in an attempt to defend his reputation.

To Phil it seemed like a concerted character assassination campaign by Britain's music press, especially when he read in NME a review of his single which called him 'The ugliest man since George Orwell'.

''And then I read a letter in Melody Maker that was nothing to do with us, it was praising Elvis Costello's *Imperial Bedroom* and praising a gig, but the bye-line from the journalist said 'It's a pity more people don't think like you because then Elvis wouldn't have to debase himself by playing with Genesis in America.'

''And I thought 'Fuck! I know Elvis, I've met him a few times, his drummer Pete Thomas is a good friend of mine, we met after the gig, they thoroughly enjoyed the gig and were blown away by the two drummers thing and we hung out and got drunk together – they didn't consider it debasing yet some hack can put a smarmy little remark like that after a letter.

''We did this gig in Philadelphia with ourselves, Blon-

die, Flock of Seagulls and Elvis; it was a carefully planned bill, everybody wanted to play with each other. But in the press it was just Elvis having a complete breakdown of taste by wanting to support Genesis!

"I thought 'This is the straw that broke the camel's back', so I wrote a letter to Melody Maker saying 'I know the people in the Elvis Costello camp, I know that he didn't consider it debasing and we all had a great time after the gig. I'm fed up with all these comments – now just get off my back.'

"The reply was 'Dear Phil, bollocks!' which I thought was an intelligent piece of journalism. Anyway, I didn't reply – I read that and thought 'forget it'."

But the saga didn't stop there.

"Then the day after my letter was printed, I got a postcard from Elvis saying 'Dear Phil, totally agree with you – will you support us on our next American tour?'. I thought 'This is unbelievable, so I wrote another letter saying 'Please – this is Elvis himself agreeing with me'. Anyway they printed that, but it's been going on for a long time . . .'

Most people might think Phil should just try to ignore such comments, which are – after all – born mostly from pathetic jealously.

And Melody Maker, in particular, has recently regarded Phil as fair game for unfair criticism, even sniping at him in their gossip column, which he finds impossible to ignore – "If I know they're there, I have to read them. You get angry, of course you do. I have to keep reminding myself that the thing is funny, probably, from somebody else's point of view.

"Someone said 'Does criticism bother you?'. Well, of course – everyone likes to be liked. If you've done something and somebody slags it off, you wouldn't relish a hundred thousand people reading it.

"Ah, maybe I'm too old" he sighed. "I don't like to see anybody clobbered on that personal level. To me, that's not music criticism. I don't mind anybody taking the music apart – if they can . . . but at the moment, the English music press and I continue to view each other with

something less than respect."

"By now, more and more people were beginning to agree with Phil. When an LP becomes someone's favourite record, it ceases to be pure entertainment: it takes on the mantle of being a treasured memento, a special present to a lover, a token of love to be cherished.

Phil Collins' fans were buying his records for more reasons than just a bouncy drum-beat and a soulful vocal, or even a touching lyric. All over the world, lovers bought Phil Collins records and identified themselves with him. They said to themselves, "Yes, I know how that feels . . ."

This shared emotion was further conveyed by the album sleeve, which featured another close-up portrait of Phil's face, but in less intimate, extreme detail than on *Face Value*.

It was an attempt to show Phil himself opening out more from the painful confines of his earlier depressing post-marriage songs.

And to emphasize both the personal nature and happier mood of the album, Phil covered the inside of the gatefold sleeve with informal polaroids. His girlfriend Jill and his children Joely and Simon were pictured next to acclaimed musicians like Daryl Stuermer and the EW&F horn section.

Some critics felt that by using photos of his kids and friends, Phil was manipulating sentiment as a cheap gimmick. "I can't help that" he replies.

"I just thought it would be an informal way of doing things. I took what I thought were humorous photos for the inside sleeve. I'm not embarrassed to have a picture of my son in a Superman costume, but I can see why it's misinterpreted.

"There is definitely a feeling of guilt about what happened to my marriage and to be purely sentimental about it – oh, I dunno . . .

"Some people find it twee. I just looked at it from the point of view that I had a son and a daughter . . . see, talking emotionally like this, I still feel embarrassed . . . but the way I looked at it, I loved my dad and I wish I had a dad."

(Phil's father, Greville, had died some years earlier.)

"And suddenly my son didn't have a dad, because my wife decided to leave me. And so, therefore, I feel *good* about putting their picture on the cover."

It was suggested that perhaps people are suspicious of a public figure prepared to reveal his innermost feelings.

"Probably" agreed Phil, "and I think that's sad. It's a drag people are embarrassed about that kind of sentimentality being shown. I wanted *Face Value* and *Hello, I Must Be Going* to be a matching set, something that felt like it was from the same bloke."

"There was no rest for Phil now. In September he'd made a brief solo appearance at the Amnesty International benefit shows. Outrageously entitled, 'The Secret Policeman's Other Ball', the concerts featured Phil (accompanied by Daryl Stuermer) alongside other stars like Sting, Pete Townshend, Eric Clapton and a whole cast of leading comedians.

"Oh my God," recalls Phil with embarrassment. "The first night was all right, but the second night I went out for a Japanese meal beforehand and had a bit too much Saki, that wine they give you. My hands felt like fists on the keyboard and I think I sung 'In The Air Tonight' completely back to front."

Barely pausing to regain his balance, Phil staggered from success to success like a drunken magician, finishing a three month Genesis tour of America and Europe and then immediately setting out on a European tour of his own, playing a set of mostly new songs in order to promote his *Hello, I Must Be Going* album and the 'You Can't Hurry Love' single.

His backing band were playing under the name of the Fabulous Jacuzzis and featured a galaxy of international master musicians – Mo Foster on bass, Peter Robinson on keyboards, both Daryl Stuermer and Chester Thompson from the Genesis live group on guitar and drums respectively plus the celebrated Earth Wind & Fire horn section.

The tour – climaxing with a run of four nights in London at the Hammersmith Odeon – was a complete triumph, as much for Collins the showman as Collins the artist. The Sounds concert review, by Jay Williams, opened with the

line "Like a pool hustler from an up-market speakeasy, The Man breezed in as if he was somebody the crowd knew personally, like somebody they always wanted to succeed".

In a way, that's exactly who Phil is. Audiences tend to identify with his character, his emotions, his *songs*, much more than they do with the songs of Genesis, where the fans are admirers (rather than participators) of the music.

So does Phil feel that his 'new' audience is different from that for Genesis?

"It is different, yeah, it's slightly older. Obviously in London, you'll get a few diehard Genesis fans, but it's not automatic. I don't really know who my fans are. I think my music can be enjoyed by suburban couples; I hope music fans think it's good music; and I hope I appeal to R'n'B fans.

"On the first tour I did, I thought I was making a complete fool of myself. I was amazed I was actually able to get through to the second night. Now I get a bit of nervous tension before I go on stage, but I'm not terrified.

"Much of this tour is geared to intimate places, I prefer them to huge arenas. My show is a bit like music hall, I really like to be close to the audience.

"I mean, I've achieved an amazing amount of satisfaction from doing my solo gigs; to have those people standing up at the end of the evening just having heard two hours of my music is a fantastic buzz because I never thought it would happen."

Part of the undoubted appeal of the Collins solo show is not only the superb music, but also the warmth and intimacy of his humour.

Relying on influences as diverse as the smooth parody of American comic Steve Martin and the British eccentricity of Monty Python and Tony Hancock, Phil virtually compered the show by donning the persona of a smarmy game-show host who insists on describing everything and everyone as either "fantastic" or "fabulous" or even both!

This element of humour was brought to the fore in a nightly ritual where Phil would introduce the horn section of "the fabulous, fabulous, fabulous Jacuzzis", overplay-

ing the compliment in an attempt to undermine the usual music business insincerity.

"There is a standard way of introducing people and everyone does it," explains Phil, "and the only way I could think of getting round it was to send it up by having it like a sleazy night-club. But that is one of the highlights of the set to me and it is a fantastic vibe when you say something and someone laughs.

"But some people don't like it – I think it was the Guardian, where Robin Denselow said it was end-of-pier humour . . . you'll never get me to stop that, because that's probably the only way I can introduce everybody. Why shouldn't people know who these great musicians are? They're playing their arse off every night! All I'm doing is taking ten minutes out to introduce them.

"I want to let everybody know who they are, whilst still maintaining some kind of flippancy."

In addition, there is also a degree of irony in that Phil himself is surrounded most of the time by people telling him just how fabulous he is! So to keep his sanity, to avoid the pitfalls of believing the more ridiculous trappings of stardom, he makes a joke of it.

"Yeah – it devalues the word," he agrees, 'in some respects, hearing that word so many times – and I deliberately say it over and over again – but still people come back-stage afterwards and say 'Fabulous . . . sorry!' so it does sink in."

But the serious point is always secondary to the sheer delight of a funny line.

"I like humour – it plays a big part in my life. I've got a lot of Tony Hancock videos that I watch with reverence. I've got the complete collection of Steve Martin – everything he's ever done."

In fact, on the inner sleeve to the album, under the heading of 'Very special thanks to' there appeared – after a long list of musicians, technicians, management personnel and friends – the names of . . . Steve Martin and Tony Hancock!

But while the humour raised a few audience laughs here and there, the most rivetting memory of those concerts

was that pulsating moment during 'In The Air Tonight' when the song exploded into a quite apocalyptic climax with both Phil and Chester Thompson thrashing away at the drums in perfect unison. Quite literally a breath-taking spectacle.

"It became a classic drum riff and I knew when I was rehearsing that I had to play it," explained Phil afterwards, "but I didn't know how I was going to play it because I didn't want to have a mike and suddenly appear behind the drums. It had to be done very well.

"Suddenly, very late in the day – almost the day before the first gig, we decided on me using the radio mike and head-set. People have high expectations of that song: it has to sound huge.

"It didn't sound right with Chester doing it: firstly, he's American and secondly, he didn't write it.

"He played the right thing but it didn't sound like it was coming from his heart. And so I had to do it myself and then it ended up with both of us doing it and it's now developed . . . I mean, when I first planned out the set I thought 'Christ, I'm the drummer but I'm only playing the drums twice!'.

"So much of the show seemed to be based on rhythm so it makes sense to have two drummers. But it's a certain type of discipline – you can't just throw them together and expect them to play.

"I'm not really aware of the power there is – I keep being told how strong it is when the two of us sit down, but I think it's good that I'm not aware of how good it is."

But even for a skilful audience manipulator like Phil, live appearances always present the possibility for disaster as he once discovered to his embarrassment in Glasgow on tour with Genesis. For once, his wonderful rapport with the audience disappeared in an instant. "I made a terrible mistake," he confesses. "I went on and said 'Glasgow, you're best audience in England!' I got booed off!"

These days, though, audiences come to see Phil Collins mainly because of his love songs, a fact which he readily admits.

"Well, 'In The Air Tonight' is almost, to a lot of people,

what I'm about — that's what they associate me with. That's how they first heard of me. They might not have liked Genesis and suddenly there was this bloke Phil Collins who had a good single out.

"I mean, at one gig there was a classic example — I was singing 'If Leaving Me Is Easy' and there was a couple in the front row and the bloke had got his arm round his girlfriend's shoulder almost as if he was saying 'Darling, don't let that happen to us'. Sometimes I think: 'Oh God, not Barry Manilow, please!' "

It almost seems that Phil hankers after the adulation and adoration reserved for younger, more athletic performers — if only to dismiss the dreaded image of becoming a cabaret crooner — but he sweeps this aside dismissively.

"No, I don't think I'm in that position. I'm just a normal, ordinary bloke. I realised long ago that female sexual worship was not likely to come my way.

'But it's extraordinary, at some gigs in the States you get quite a few screamers. And you just think 'God, who's walked on stage?' But Jill goes everywhere with me, so they don't get very far."

11

GENESIS INTO THE FUTURE

In the summer of 1983, when Phil reunited with Tony and Mike, they discovered that they all still had the desire to make music *together* despite the comparative success of their respective solo records – Phil Collins' *Hello I Must Be Going*, Tony Banks' *Acting Very Strange* and Mike Rutherford's *The Fugitive*. All three records, ironically, featured Genesis bassist Daryl Stuermer who never appears on Genesis albums, since Mike Rutherford takes care of all guitar duties in the studio!

Recording again at The Farm, they soon had enough material for their fifteenth LP, to be released in October 1983 and simply entitled *Genesis*.

This was teeming with great melodies and memorable choruses; all nine tracks mixing swirling melodrama with heartbeat rhythms, worthy of more modern groups such as Tears For Fears and Simple Minds. By now, the band had developed a unique style of blending together their own individual musical inputs to create a forever-shifting group sound.

Gone were the petty jealousies and self-doubts that marred earlier albums; the group spirit was now so strong that they were happy to credit all composition merely to Genesis, an unknown occurrence since Gabriel had quit.

(By contrast, this album ironically marked the return of the insert lyric sheet!)

But by now they were all agreed that the final track and its musical content were all that mattered, not who wrote

which line of lyric or snatch of melody.

The hit single 'Mama' (released a couple of weeks before the album itself) was a case in point, as Mike Rutherford pointed out at the time in an interview with Sounds.

"Our problem in the past has been that very often the best stuff we've done on an album hasn't stood a chance as a single because it's been so wrong in that context. So we've put out songs that I've liked and have worked well as singles but have simply not been the best songs we've had at the time.

"But 'Mama' is, I think, one of the best songs on the new album and is at the same time very much what Genesis is all about. To have a hit with a song which is six minutes long is also very exciting."

Hugh Fielder's astute album review in Sounds picks out 'Mama' as the best track: "definitely the most vivid song with its superb build-up to the fierce, raw and reverberating pitch sustained by Phil's wicked laughs and increasingly white soul vocals."

One of the most interesting tracks is 'Home By The Sea', which Rutherford describes as "A song I could have seen us doing six or seven years ago, but now we've done it in a way that makes it sound even better".

It is immediately followed at the end of side one by the quasi-instrumental 'Second Home By The Sea' with its brief lyrical reprise, which Fielder terms 'a storming slab of marching pomp' – accurately reflecting its aura of classic mid-seventies Genesis – and sums up their advance by explaining 'essentially, what's happened is that the traditional Genesis riffs that used to spread over minutes have now been compressed into seconds.'

Howver, Steve Sutherland of Melody Maker didn't agree with that at all: he reckoned that 'the album as a whole flirts with funk; but it's diversity without commitment . . .' and called it 'appalling'.

In particular, he savaged the jokey calypso of 'Illegal Alien' as 'blatantly insensitive', 'offensively inept' and 'smug indolence, obnoxious trifling. They might as well be singing about rhubarb for all the concern or insight they show.'

The problem with 'Illegal Alien' lies not so much with its lyrics, which attempt to portray the plight of Mexicans so desperate to reach the 'promised land' of America that they'd willingly trade their sisters for a passport.

Even Sutherland conceded that Genesis were trying to treat the problem in a semi-serious manner with lines such as the following:

'Consideration for your fellow man,
Wouldn't hurt anybody, sure fits in with my plan'

and

'I've got a sister who'd be willing to oblige
She will do anything now to help me get to the
    outside'.

But it was the whole style of the song's presentation that seemed at best inconsidered and at worst downright offensive. It was almost as though the famous Genesis schoolboy humour had simply gone too far and the band themselves hadn't recognised the thin line between parody and racial ridicule. Certainly the passing references to "a bottle of tequila and a new pack of cigarettes" and the photograph of the three band members made up to look like Mexicans merely reinforced the prejudiced view of the stereotyped unemployed peasant selling clothes pegs and getting drunk.

Much more successful in concept and execution were the beautiful anguish of 'Taking It All Too Hard' – featuring one of Phil's most soulfully emotional vocals ever – and the reflective pop of 'Silver Rainbow', which begins as a pastoral love song ('Winter follows springtime/Morning ends the day/Beyond the silver rainbow') and ends up as a bitter-sweet ballad about sexual desire with a final line of 'you won't know if you're coming or going'.

The main success of the *Genesis* album lay in its melodies which all had a comforting, familiar feel about them (while sounding radically different from the band's previous work) and this was then emphasised by the

simplicity and repetitiveness of the choruses, which mostly consisted of one key line being repeated anywhere from twice ('Taking It All To Hard') to eight times, as on 'Illegal Alien'.

This simple, yet very effective, new style was shown to its best effect by the chart success of 'Mama'. And it was due to the fact that, according to Mike Rutherford, 'We're always looking for change. Since we originally started with very complicated songs, then the only way we could go is in this direction – we couldn't have got much more complex! We probably tried too hard in those days, but now we take a much more relaxed approach.

"I've felt we've been tied down by our history, it's often felt like a weight around our neck having to keep recording albums in a similar vein. And that's something we've tried to break away from . . ." Tony: "First and foremost in my mind is the music; once we finish one album, I'm thinking about the next. I find it very exciting that people want to hear our music – whether in Hong Kong or Barnstaple. I feel it's a unifying force, something that brings people together rather than pushes them apart, which I'm definitely in favour of.

"We've been such a slow growing band but we've never stopped growing since the moment we started. Almost every album has sold more than its predecessor. And there can't be many groups who have managed to do that over ten or eleven years."

In November, Genesis once more flew to America for another massive tour finishing on 20th February the following year in San Francisco – seventy-two concerts from coast-to-coast . . . a far cry from their first two solitary concerts back in 1972!

This was immediately followed by five successive nights at Birmingham's NEC. These shows were notable for two reasons: firstly, they were the only European concerts by Genesis in 1984 at all, and second, the last two evenings were special charity shows. Inevitably, all five shows sold out within hours of the tickets going on sale.

Faced with such overwhelming success (both artistic and commercial) the critics once more sent up the cry

"How much longer can Genesis last?"

"I don't see why it can't go on for a while," says Phil. "We all get on better than we've ever done. We laugh a lot. There is a lot of humour in Genesis that gets overlooked."

As if on cue, Mike jokes "People make you feel like a bank when they ask how secure Genesis is. They like to feel Genesis is going to carry on forever, when the truth is it's as secure or insecure as it ever was."

Phil nods in agreement. "People are always asking us 'Well, you've played New York's Madison Square Garden now, what's your ambition?' – well, to play TWO nights at Madison Square Garden. To sell it out in an hour instead of six hours.

"There are always gonna be new ambitions – I remember a gig where Genesis were playing with Graham Bell at Aberystwyth University and we broke down three times on the way there, arrived too late to play, and broke down four times on the way back. I fondly recollect that story but at the same time, it couldn't have been much fun at the time; it's a pain in the arse when you keep breaking down.

"But there's no way that you hit a plateau and that's it. I still get the same buzz out of the gigs I'm doing now as I did then.

Even all the attention and adulation heaped on Phil Collins – both as Genesis front-man and as a solo star – doesn't seem to affect the group spirit.

"I'd like to think that it's the doing of it, the playing of the game, rather than the winning . . ." explained Phil. "I feel frustrated for Tony and Mike that they can't be seen outside of what people think they are."

But certainly the others – especially Tony – didn't feel in any way inferior partners. As Banks explained to Hot Press magazine: "I've never made any secret of the fact that I was not a great fan of Phil's first album – I think the second one is much better. And so I don't really see any connection between his stuff and ours apart from obviously the drum sound and the singing.

"If I felt that Phil was dominating the band, there's no way I'd still be in Genesis because I'm a hopeless person to try and dominate."

This was something of which Phil was well aware. "Mike and Tony take the mickey all the time – 'Oh Phil, your single is only at Number Three, what are you going to do now?' or 'What a shame, it's only sold 400,000 this time, how on earth will you manage?'. They bring me down to earth!

"When I'm with Genesis, the most important thing is Genesis – and when I'm producing an album, that's the most important thing. It's really whatever is on at the time.

"You put on different hats. I love playing different music and that's why I spread myself around.

"But I couldn't imagine not being part of Genesis."

However this is just the situation that many many people – critics and fans alike – continually suggest.

"It's unfortunate that every time I do an interview, I'm pushed into defending Genesis," agrees Phil. "Journalists can't understand why I stay with the band when I'm so successful on my own, or why – in fact – the band is still around.

"They feel we've been around for so long that we must have outlived our usefulness. But you see, we write music for ourselves – we don't write for our audience or our critics at all.

"I enjoy playing with the band and we all enjoy writing with each other, and we do it all infrequently enough for it to be fun. We do an album every couple of years, that's what it boils down to. There's no legal or binding thing between us except that we actually enjoy doing it.

"There are faults with Genesis but you stay with a group until the faults are rectified. When there are no more faults to rectify, you leave or the group splits up. You certainly try to make it better – that's why you keep doing albums.

"Providing the majority of members are still the original members, you've still got whatever it is – the chemistry, the identifiable sound or style – it's still there.

"When Steve left, there were still the three of us – and I consider myself to be an original member. Actually, I'm still called 'the new boy' . . . and I've been here eleven years!"

But Phil isn't blind to criticisms of Genesis and appreci-

129

ates why some people still don't like the music.

"I don't want to kick our fans in the teeth – but at the same time, I'm sure they don't like Genesis for the same reasons I like it. They like Genesis for maybe the area of music I like least in it.

"I always feel that if people don't like Genesis, it's because they haven't given it enough time. Because as far as I'm concerned, I like good music and *I* like what we're doing. So I can't understand why other people don't. I don't think Genesis is the perfect group, but we're still trying to get it right."

Is that what keeps you going, that striving?

"Yeah – I've been asked lots of times why didn't I leave the band, but I'll stay in the group until we get it right, until we deliver something that I feel 'YEAHHH!'."

Already, Genesis have started work on their new album – their sixteenth, after a decade and a half together. As yet untitled, it is due for release in Spring 1986.

"Every time you do an album, you think it's the best and when someone asks which is my favourite album, I say 'the new one'."

Chapter

12

INTERNATIONAL SUCCESS

At the time of *Face Value*, Phil had written a tune called 'How Can You Sit There?', "But I didn't use it because I found I had one too many slow songs, and that was my least favourite. Then it nearly went on *Hello I Must Be Going*, but I found I had enough songs for that too!"

Then during the 1983/84 Genesis tour of America, Phil was approached by film director Taylor Hackford – best known for 'An Officer And A Gentleman' – who asked him to write a song for his new film, 'Against All Odds'.

Phil was shown a rough cut of the film and agreed to come up with something. "Being in the middle of a tour, I didn't really have time to write a new song, so I sent him a demo of this and he loved it! Then I added the words to the tune, so lyrically it was written for the film.

"I didn't have time to produce it either, so I drafted in Arif Mardin and said 'I know you'd be able to handle it, I want you to arrange the strings' – because he's a brilliant arranger."

Phil had long admired Mardin's smooth production on classic records by such diverse artists as Aretha Franklin, Brook Benton, Roberta Flack, Leo Sayer, Carly Simon and Hall & Oates.

And he had even witnessed this incomparable talent at first hand when he arranged the string accompaniment for 'If Leaving Me Is Easy' on *Face Value*. He knew he was the only man for the job.

So one day between Genesis gigs, Phil flew to New York

to meet Mardin and the two of them recorded the backing track with a full orchestra and a piano player, before Phil left to rejoin the Genesis tour with the problem of how to find time to write the words.

Two weeks later Arif Mardin arrived in Los Angeles where Phil recorded the drums and the vocals. "And then I asked him to mix it. He sent me a copy of the mixes and he'd be on the phone while I was listening to it, and I'd be saying 'a little less echo on the drums, a bit more on the voice' and the whole thing was done like that. He produced it and we kept liaising.

"To me, it was such a different way of working that I never took it seriously. Considering it was my only Number One record in America, it was made in a very roundabout haphazard fashion!"

Even when he's having Number One hits in the American pop charts, Phil always maintains that his roots are in black music – especially early Tamla Motown and R'n'B. And also the Beatles, which is why he'd chosen to cover 'Tomorrow Never Knows' on *Face Value*.

"I guess my background comes from listening to Ringo. I've got a tape of unreleased Beatles stuff which has just surfaced in the States, and the drumming is just fantastic. It reminds me of just how good Ringo was.

"So there's a bit of me in that, right next to a bit of Bernard Purdie or (EW&F drummer) Freddie White. It's that combination that adds up to something a little different."

It was these sort of influences that led to him to work on the solo album by EW&F vocalist Philip Bailey, which started out as a smooth soul record and ended up as a strange hybrid of rock and R'n'B, of which Phil is really proud.

"Originally, when Philip talked to me about doing the album, we said we'd do it in London, because he wanted me to give him what I do best – which means musicians of my choice."

Phil picked sidemen he knew he could trust – guitarist Daryl Stuermer from the Genesis touring band and keyboard player Peter Robinson from Phil's own back-up live

group.

"And Philip said he'd like to use Nathan East as bass player. I said 'Great, I've never played with Nathan; he's a wonderful bass player'.

"We spent the week rehearsing at my house. Peter Robinson, when he's sounding things out, doesn't play with much feel. He was just trying to get the chords right. And Philip wasn't happy with that. I said 'Ignore it, it'll be okay. Just trust me'. But he was still a little on edge."

To keep Bailey happy, Collins agreed to a new keyboard-player and they drafted in Seth Wilson, who used to play with Chaka Khan.

For the next couple of days, the atmosphere in the studio was decidedly uneasy because Phil felt rather isolated as Philip Bailey was relying more and more on Nathan for advice and encouragement. And this feeling of alienation was further increased by the style of the actual music they were rehearsing – traditional R'n'B, Earth Wind & Fire type songs – which would have been more suited to the studio atmosphere generated in Los Angeles.

"So there I was, trying to get these songs sound like they had been done in LA and they weren't using me at my best. It was like, 'Hey, I'm supposed to be the producer here!'

"Eventually I said to George (Massenberg), 'Listen George, I'll play on this album, but as soon as the playing's done, you can carry on with Philip because I don't really believe I'm really wanted here. I don't think I'm really needed, because Philip has been confiding more in Nathan than in me.'

"Well, that got back to Philip and Nathan – and Nathan really wanted to play with me, to do this project together. So he said to Philip one night at the hotel, 'Listen, you're not taking advantage of the situation. You've got Phil, you've got the studio. Let's use him for what we're paying him for.'

"So Philip came in and we talked about it, He said what we should do is make an album of what we're best at, as opposed to trying to make an R'n'B album. And suddenly, the thing changed completely, and we went full power into

this. All the tracks were great fun after that.''

It seems much of the problem had been American radio DJs and programmers (who have a lot of power and influence over the record-buying public) warning Bailey off straying from his black roots. He'd actually been told ''Listen, boy, you to go London, you don't make a white, honky album. You make an R'n'B album. Otherwise, we ain't gonna play it.''

Collins became aware of the problem and sympathised with Bailey's dilemma: ''He's thinking 'What am I gonna do? I want to play with Phil, but if I make a pretty, white album, they're not gonna play it.'

''It's amazing that this goes on, because racism is always thought of as coming from our end. But it's like when 'I Missed Again' came out, all the the white stations said 'It's got horns on it – we can't play it'. And the black stations wouldn't play it bacause I'm not black . . .''

But after they'd discussed the problem, the Bailey/Collins collaboration gained momentum as they began to enjoy working together.

''We just went for the songs we liked. They were the traditional R'n'B songs like 'Show You The Way To Love' an 'For Every Heart That's Been Broken', and a few English songs like 'Children Of The Ghetto' and 'Time Is A Woman'.

''But the very last thing that we did was 'Easy Lover'. Philip said we should write something together, so the group got together and we wrote the stuff. I wrote the words, and we did a take of it one night after we'd written it in the studio.

''We wanted to record it again the next day, but when we heard the take that we'd done the night before, we said 'That's the one! Let's keep it.'

''It's a very good single but there's been a lot of prejudice around it. A lot of black radio stations wouldn't play it because Philip was singing with a white man. They said he should have sounded blacker.

''I know what that feels like. In England, Tony Blackburn won't play my single because I'm a white artist playing soul music and he thinks that isn't right.''

But even without certain DJs giving it their full support, 'Easy Lover' became UK Number One – partly with the help of an informal 'home movie'-type video portraying the cool dude Bailey and slightly dishevelled Collins clowning around in rehearsal for the song. It was typical Phil Collins; when faced with the smooth sophistication of a master soul performer like Bailey, he still came up trumps by adopting the role of Mr Average!

"One of the things that I'm kind of proud of – though it's not been a vendetta I've been on – but with things like Philip and me teaming up, this has meant that he's broken into MTV."

The chart success of the 'Easy Lover' duet then paved the way for Bailey's next single, 'Chinese Wall', which was also a hit.

"And for me," adds Collins, "it means my records now get played on R'n'B stations. So really, these collaborations – between McCartney and Michael Jackson, and him and Stevie Wonder – they have the obvious advantages, in terms of getting rid of things musicians don't think about generally.

"As a producer and co-artist on 'Easy Lover', I was very proud of the fact that it got to Number Three in the R'n'B charts. That was great for me to get over to that area, and since then, people like Al Jarreau and Tina Turner and Ronnie Spector have been interested and have asked me if I wanted to produce them. To me, that's really getting somewhere."

In many ways, 1984 was a year of collaborations for Phil Collins. After all, he didn't record a new LP either by himself or with Genesis (who only played a handful of live dates after recovering from their huge US trek) – and so he had more free time than he might have imagined.

Back in 1982, Phil had told this author "I'd like to do an album with Clapton actually," and two years later this wish became reality with the latter's album, *Behind The Sun*.

It seemed to most people that Clapton, despite being one of the best guitarists in the world, was – quite bluntly – well past his best, having lost the hunger for success.

"I don't think he's lost the hunger for it," corrected Collins. "I just think there's another side to him. There was a period, up until recently when he'd been coasting a bit because he'd surrounded himself with friends – he's told me before that he prefers to be in a group rather than be the leader and I think maybe the people he was with weren't strong enough to be part of the group with him."

Perhaps Collins could provide the necessary firm hand tempered by the softness of genuine affection. As Eric himself says "Phil and I have been friends for quite a while now, going back to the mid-seventies. There's always been a mutual admiration club between us.

"I approached Phil a couple of years ago and asked if he'd consider producing an album with me. He's a very busy man, he really works non-stop all year round. But it turned out he had a gap in his schedule, so we went off to Montserrat."

The album was recorded, then Phil and Eric went back to London to finish mixing and the final product was presented to the record company, Warner Brothers.

But even the words, 'produced by Phil Collins' still don't guarantee total satisfaction – at least, not among music business executives!

After hearing the finished album, Warner Brothers management complained that there wasn't enough guitar on it. So they contacted Clapton and told him they weren't happy with the LP. "They said they didn't think it had enough hit material for airplay as it stood and would I consider going back into the studio.

"I was a little bit upset, but I could see their point. When Phil and I made the record, we decided it would be the first real personal, intimate record I ever made, showing sides of me people had never seen before. The record company didn't wholeheartedly agree with that!"

Warners subsequently replaced several of Collins produced tracks by others recorded with Ted Templeman and Lenny Waronker. Phil was furious. "Warner Brothers said 'There's no guitar on it – it's meant to be an Eric Clapton album.' Because everybody thinks that an Eric Clapton album has got to have guitar solos all over it!

"He played on 'If Leaving Me Is Easy' and people would come up to me and say 'He didn't play on that! There's no guitar solo!'. But he's in the background, if you listen. On this album he was experimenting with the Roland guitar synth, so a lot of the stuff that you think is synthesiser is really guitar, like 'Never Make You Cry'.

"He was trying to push himself into another area and everybody was saying 'Get back there!'

"But after Warners heard Eric's album, nobody called me with their comments. I heard all these negative comments second-hand, but nothing positive. That really annoyed me.

"To me, it encapsulates what their attitude towards Eric is when you hear them quoted as saying he's in the same market-place as Duran Duran.

"*Another Ticket* and *Money And Cigarettes*, I thought, had just left the music laying on the record. It didn't jump out. People had written him off, thinking 'Oh, that was Eric ten years ago.' I wanted to show that he still *did* do it, and that his enthusiasm for the music is still as much as it was. I think the thing was that he was surrounded by people who would say 'Yeah, that's great' when it wasn't.

"But far be it from me to say 'You can do better', because when I got in there . . . like the first time I pressed the button and said 'That was a good solo, Eric. Why don't you try another one?' You just don't do that. I mean, I *had* to do that, I was paid to do that, but it's a very tricky situation the first time you do it."

Besides producing the album, Phil also played on several tracks, while long-time Clapton sideman Jamie Oldaker drummed on the others . . . all except for *Behind The Sun* itself, on which Phil and Jamie teamed up.

"Yeah, that's the only time on the record with the two of them together," says Clapton. "And it is pretty big, I must admit."

But not everything in the studio ran smoothly, and the guitar work on 'Same Old Blues' is fired up sheer anger, as Eric admits. "For the first time ever, there was a bit of aggravation between Phil and me. I don't want to say what it was, it's too personal. But we did fall out and I told him

all about it through my playing. Yeah, there was a lot of angst in there."

But such occasional flare-ups are all part and parcel of the producer's lot. He has to be more than simply the technician responsible for the sound and feel of the music: he has to be confidante, advisor, dictator, nurse and best friend all in one. And Phil is one of the best, despite his modest denials.

"I don't really produce records; I help people make their own records. Philip Bailey's thing, for instance – we just got a band together, learned the songs, and put them down.

"But I've had lots of offers from various people," he admits. "The Nolans sounded interesting but there wasn't time to do it, Air Supply . . . who I wasn't interested in, but again I was flattered – I'm flattered if any one asks me to produce them.

"There's also a singer called Eugene Wallace. I played on a couple of albums of his in the mid-seventies; he's just resurfaced and he's got a fabulous voice. There's lots of things I've been offered, but it's a question of time."

Amongst others who have requested his expertise as producer are Cliff Richard and Pete Townshend. In fact, at one time Phil even asked Pete Townshend whether he could join The Who!

"When Moony died, I was doing some sessions with Townshend and I said 'If you need a drummer I'll make myself available', and we got on very well, but he'd already asked Kenny Jones."

One fascinating collaboration that didn't actually occur but at one time seemed a possibility was Phil Collins and Julian Lennon.

"He wanted me to produce his album and he gave me a tape of two songs; it was rough but it's amazing how much he sounds like his dad.

"He was surrounded by these four blokes and they came to the Genesis gigs at Hammersmith every night, four blokes . . . one was younger than Julian and was introduced to me as his business adviser, there was another guy who was talking to me about Julian while Julian was

there and he was saying 'Well Julian's doing this and he wants to do that' – and I was just wondering if Julian had a tongue! At the end of the evening, I called Julian over and said 'Listen, I loved your dad, I'd love to help you, anything I can do . . . but if you want me to do it, you ask me – get rid of these people!'

"He said 'I know what you mean' and that was the last thing I heard. I've got a number where I can get hold of him . . . but it almost seems that he's there doing what he's doing because of who his dad was instead of having a burning ambition to do it. And I know that he has said that Yoko has told him the same thing – 'Find yourself before you do anything'. I'm sure he's a very sweet guy, but he's got a lot on his shoulders."

Since that conversation took place, Julian Lennon has indeed taken time to discover his own values and has subsequently had worldwide success with his *Valotte* LP and 'Too Late For Goodbye' single.

But for Phil, there is no shortage of artists anxious to secure his production services.

"Some people ask me what on earth I'm doing producing an old blues man like Eric Clapton or working with Adam Ant, but I love variety. Music is a common denominator.

"I'm sure Adam Ant asked me to work to produce him because Frida's single 'I know There's Something Going On' did so well in the US.

"It doesn't really bother me whether I'm working with Robert Plant, Frida, Genesis or whoever. It's all different and I've never felt that I've got to be tied down to just one thing. Maybe it's because I get asked to do so many different types of things.

"There's enough room with Genesis for me to go and do all these different things."

Are there any other artists Phil would like to produce?

"Well, Darryl Hall and I have talked about doing something – I'd played on a Robert Fripp track which he sang on, so we had something to talk about. But I think that is a collaboration, it's not like me actually producing an album by him – it's a question of sitting down together

and talking about ideas, so I think that's a long-term thing.

"And Maurice White was someone else that I've been in contact with, and his manager wants to get us together – which is great for me. To get together with someone that I admire so much would be great . . . and Stephen Bishop, I would love to do an album with him – I just like to work closely with people that I like."

Because he's such as music fan himself, Phil enjoys working with a wide variety of other musicians and singers. In fact, he doesn't have enough hours in the day to fit everything into his overcrowded schedule.

"I work all the time because people ask me to. I'm pretty flattered when people like Clapton want me to work for them, but it's not work to me – it's good fun. I hate hanging about doing nothing.

"I love what I do – apart from my own stuff and Genesis, which I could never leave, Tina Turner and Al Jarreau want me to produce them. I don't know if I'll have the time, but you can't just refuse a chance like that because you're a bit tired, can you?"

13

NO JACKET REQUIRED

Never stopping for a moment, Phil Collins the producer metamorphosed once more into Phil Collins the solo artist. The time had come, he felt, to get down to making some serious dance music – partly because that's what he loves, but also to show that he wasn't settling into comfortable middle-age and growing further away from his audience.

"I still have the same youthful energy," he chuckles. "Before my last tour, I went for the usual medical – and the doctor passed me 100 per cent fit! I was pleasantly surprised.

"I get the same buzz out of what I'm doing and with this new album, I wanted to make a pretty fast dancey sort of record."

And so, in May 1985, Phil Collins' third solo alum, *No Jacket Required*, was released.

"I think I've been labelled as Phil Collins the balladeer for a couple of years now. But I love ballads. 'Ballads' is a terrible word, isn't it? Makes me sound like Barry Manilow. I love slow songs. Although I've done a lot of work since my first album, I'm still quite closely associated with it."

But *No Jacket Required* was a bold step away from the melancholy piano chords and haunting love-torn ballads. It showed the influences of modern black pop, ranging from energetic disco of Michael Jackson to the outrageous electronic R'n'B of Prince.

"This album draws on so much more. I set myself the target of writing things that I hadn't done much before. I wanted it to be more dance-orientated.

"So I set up some up-tempo stuff, things that got me excited rhythmically, and I thrashed about on the keyboard until I got something that musically excited me as well – that's how 'Sussudio' came about."

This track, despite being a successful hit single, has been unfavourably compared to Prince's hit '1999', to which it bears more than a passing resemblance. One UK disc jockey even played the two tracks back-to-back and discovered that they share virtually the same rhythm!

"Well, I wanted to make a dance record," explains Phil wearily, "so I listened to a few of my favourites and took their tempos. Keyboardist David Frank insisted that the synth sounded nothing like '1999' and said his bass part would alter everything. So I took his word for it – but recording 'Sussidio' is the worst possible thing I could have done!"

Of course, when released as a single, 'Sussudio' became a chart hit in its own right and again Phil made such a wonderfully low-key humorous video that all allegations of plagiarism – whether intentional or accidental – were soon forgotten.

As with all of his promotional videos, 'Sussudio' plays to Collins strengths. He's never been tempted to create elaborate story-lines to depict the lyric, preferring instead to concentrate firstly on the performance of the song and secondly to add lighter elements of humour where possible. On this occasion, the pounding rhythmic force of the song is emphasised by having the band play in a dingy pub in front of an apathetic audience. But when that whiplash 'Sussudio' beat starts cracking, the whole place is transformed into wild elation!

This sudden emphasis on dance music owes much to Phil's new-found domestic happiness – "It's because I'm remarried, and I guess the ballad side of me is not coming out so much. Even 'One More Night', the lyrics there are rather more optimistic in a warm way, rather than depressing in a negative way. I just found that I wasn't writing

ballads.

"And I want to try new things – which is why I'd never do another Motown cover. Of course, as soon as you've had a Number One hit, the tendency is to think 'OK, that's what the people want to hear – OK, that's what I'll do!'

"But that's a good enough reason for me *not* to want to do it. I certainly don't want to get stuck in the role of balladeer. I think Stephen Bishop is a good example of what happens then. He had a couple of hits with ballads and suddenly he can't do anything else. People don't want to know about his doing anything else."

It was also obvious that Phil had been spurred on by the recent revival in black music which had witnessed long-neglected soul acts suddenly scoring chart hits: undeniable talents such as Womack & Womack, Prince and Ashford & Simpson. This, combined with Phil's lasting passion for sixties R'n'B, acted as a catalyst for his own renewed emphasis on rhythmic importance.

"Occasionally I listen to the radio – but if I put a record on at home, it's more likely to be a Beatles album or an Earth Wind & Fire album or *Aretha Franklin's Greatest Hits*.

"I prefer that kind of music – R'n'B and black music in general, or something like Weather Report."

The Beatles influence, to which Phil readily admitted, was again in evidence, especially on 'Only You Know And I Know' where the chorus bore an uncanny resemblance to 'Things We Said Today' which had originally been the B-side of 'Hard Day's Night' – the film in which Phil made a fleeting appearance!

The Lyrics to that song also broke new barriers as Phil skilfully combined passion and cynical humour to deal with heartache from a new angle using bitter-sweet observations rather than merely relying on pathos.

'Sometimes I know you gotta be cruel,
Be cruel to be kind,
When I ask you what you see in me,
You say our love is blind!'

No Jacket Required showed certain changes in mood but maintained a consistent style and approach. His voice had never sounded better – whether roaring on brash dance

numbers like 'I Don't Wanna Know' or carressing the emotions of softer tracks like 'One More Night' – and much of this was due to teaming up again with engineer Hugh Padgham.

Their mercurial collaboration continued to function as a blend of blind intuition and precise experience.

"I'm not very technical at all," admits Phil gleefully. "I'll say 'a bit more top please!' whereas they'll say 'another 400Hz' or something – it's all garbage to me. I'm glad that somebody knows what they're talking about!'

In fact, Phil is being rather too modest, but explains the intricate working relationship he now enjoys with master-engineer Hugh Padgham.

"The credits on this album should really be 'co-produced by Phil Collins and Hugh Padgham, directed by Phil Collins and photographed by Hugh Padgham – I have the ideas, but I give the problems to him! I say 'This is what I think it should sound like, you tell me how to do it.''

In fact, the sleeve credit showed a simple 'produced by Phil Collins and Hugh Padgham', but even this was a public acknowledgement of just how vital Hugh is in attaining the required studio sound. Many lesser artists would gladly – and greedily – have accepted all the acclaim for themselves.

To an extent, though, the third LP sounded quite similar to the first and second; a blend of heartache and ballads and up-tempo dance tunes – with more emphasis on the latter this time – with that thundrous Collins drum sound.

But every Phil Collins project throws up its surprises and *No Jacket* was no exception! There, blending in with Phil's own soulful vocals on 'Take Me Home' were a trio of highly distinctive singers in their own right: Sting, Helen Terry and Peter Gabriel.

As before, the songs were intensely personal and emotionally moving. For Phil, it's almost impossible to separate his public career from his private, personal life. 'Doesn't Anybody Stay Together Any More?', for instance, prompted a lot a speculation about the inspiration for the lyrics.

This time, though, it wasn't Phil's own divorce that acted as artistic inspiration.

"Hugh Padgham, Tony Smith and I were sitting in the studio together. Tony had just been divorced and we were thinking about all of our friends who had split with their partners in 1984. We started counting and the list was incredible – about two dozen people.

"Some of them were my best friends, and some of them very close. Eric and Patti (Clapton) are now back together. Thank God – because they helped me through my long, low period. And I'd look up to them as the ideal couple. But you see that fall apart and you think 'My God, doesn't anybody stay together any more?'

"The rhythm was based on a thing that I did on that Gabriel album, a track that I though was one of the best things he ever did, but that he never used. I just took the drum part – which was mine (laughs), I wrote it – and did a song around it.

"There's a humorous side to that song, really. It's not actually 'WHY DOESN'T ANYBODY STAY TOGETHER?" It's more like 'What's the matter, doesn't anybody stay together any more?''. It was meant to be like that, rather than relating to my own personal circumstances. I *was* that soldier – but suddenly my friends were dropping like flies around me."

For someone who made his reputation as a songwriter by exploring the pain of his own marriage break-up, Phil could run the risk of being called a hypocrite by even dreaming up a title such as 'Doesn't Anybody Stay Together Anymore?' But, in fact, his views on marriage, morality and romance remain surprisingly conservative – especially when the matter of divorce and infidelity is mentioned.

"Before the sixties, anything like tht was brushed under the carpet once it was found out. Whereas in the sixties, everybody learned that if you don't want it, don't do it. In the Victorian days, you got married and – whether you wanted to or not – you stayed with your wife. And if you wanted a mistress, you did it as subtly as possible.

"But it's just escalated from then, to the point now

where people get married because they think that's it, and then they realise, really, that's *not* it. Then they get a divorce.

"So the fatality rate is very high. I know that to a certain extent I was relieved when I found Jill. I mean, I went to school with Andrea – it's not like we didn't know each other. But chemistry-wise, Jill knows exactly what I need to do with myself. I love to work – and she knows that. We have a laugh about it and then she says 'We should go on holiday' – and I know we *should* go on holiday!

"You only get one crack at the whip, you only get one life. And you might as well do it the way you want to do it. To be shackled, to be manacled together in a situation – and, again, I don't want it to sound like I *was* manacled – but to be put into a situation straight away . . . you're supposed to be *happy* when you get married. You choose to be with this person because you enhance each other. If that isn't there, then your best thing is to get out."

"But I don't want people just to think of me as some bloke who will never forget about being divorced.

"Unfortunately, it's relevant because I didn't write any good songs before – but now Jill thinks why the hell do I keep talking about it?"

By 1985, Phil Collins had ceased to become merely a solo artist and musician, he'd become that most public of properties, a PERSONALITY!

"I've done three solo albums and every one has my face on the cover! So, if I'm a bit more recognisable, it's my own fault," he laughs. "I wanted it that way because my albums are such personal things; especially *Face Value* which was virtually a diary.

"The next album *Hello, I Must Be Going* was similar, but with more of a 'coming out of the dark' feeling, so we added that very bright blue background, which was a theme we continued through the last tour, when the stage set was entirely blue.

"Then with the new one, *No Jacket Required*, the music is much hotter – so I was trying to think of a way of depicting that, and we came up with the bright red lighting on my face – and I'm sweating! Clever stuff, eh? It all ties in with the title, and it's a continuation of the series.

14

THE MAN BEHIND THE MUSIC

In August 1984, Phil Collins remarried, eventually making an honest woman of his girlfriend Jill Tavelman, after they'd already been living together for four years.

Both of them had been anxious not to rush into marriage: Phil could be excused for thinking of the old adage 'Once bitten, twice shy' but he had no doubts whatsoever about Jill being jealous of his career – after all they'd met on a Genesis tour and she'd witnessed with delight his emergence as a solo performer of international stature.

"The thing is," explained Phil, "She's been in the music business so she knows what to expect."

The wedding decision was broken to the world press by Phil's personal assistant Carol Willis who said: "Having gone through one broken marriage, Phil wanted to make sure that this time he'd chosen the right person.

"He knows Jill is absolutely right and they're very much in love. But Phil is such a workaholic that he won't take a honeymoon immediately. They will probably go away in the autumn – somewhere hot, sunny and romantic."

Away from all the transatlantic flights, videos, hit singles and sell-out concert tours, Collins leads a quiet life. Phil and Jill now live in a huge house in Surrey, a highly desirable property.

"This house wasn't expensive when I bought it, but it's worth double what I paid for it, so it's a good investment. One side of the house is a century old while the other side

dates back even further than that.

"I don't think it's haunted, but I recall there was a strange odour that used to follow you around from room to room. But I've spent a lot of time here on my own and I've never felt anything evil.

"But it's only Jill who's got it to be like a home, because she's a lady, y'know?"

Not only a home, though. The house also features an upstairs room that has been converted to a small but modern studio, where Phil lays down demos of his songs. This is where he recorded most of *Face Value*.

"It's a good job they changed the beams in the floor when they modernised it. If this hadn't been done, then I'm told the piano would have gone straight through the floor. It might have killed somebody."

Downstairs most of the walls are finished in pine, except the kitchen where the walls have been stripped to reveal the original brick-work. Upstairs one small room is decorated with floating clouds and a rainbow: a reminder of Phil's missing children, Simon and Joely, who now live in Vancouver, Canada, with their mother.

"Before they went away," recalls Phil, "I saw them every weekend, but I still enjoy their company for two months in the summer because I make sure I don't work and that I've got time for them.

"I phone them up every week and we talk for about three-quarters of an hour. The bills are tremendous. I have to blot out the fact that I'm not with them all the time. I enjoy my children incredibly – I really wish they could live with me but they live with their mum and that's the way it is.

"But when I see them I'm a total dad and we all go crazy. Joely is my adopted daughter, she knows I'm not her real dad – but they're both my children as far as I'm concerned.

"My son wants to be a drummer and he has got a lot of talent. He's a big Van Halen fan, but they like different things each week. I'll encourage him if he wants to go into the business, but I won't push him. It'll be up to him.

"It's funny, though, they look up at a poster of me or see me on television and yell 'Hey look, there's dad'!"

The pain of his broken marriage and his absent children still hurts, not least of all because he has had to endure most of the painful experiences in the public glare provided by the world's media.

And equally, his ex-wife Andrea feels that she has been unfairly treated by being portrayed in Phil's songs as a heartless adultress. Recently she attemped to redress the balance by successfully demanding that Rolling Stone print an apology to her after a cover feature on Phil had repeated certain derogatory comments from Collins.

Phil is quick to explain.

"I spent a week with the writer when I was working on *No Jacket Required* and you say things in conversation you never imagine are going to end up in print. She was fed up with people reading about my side of the story as she has her version, of course.

"As it is, I get an amazing amount of flak from her: everytime a new song comes out, she has to listen to it if it's on the radio in Canada where she now lives. And the kids have to listen to it too . . ."

Of course, sometimes the pressure gets to everyone, even a placid personality like Collins, who has been dubbed pop's 'Mr. Nice Guy'.

At the end of his last world tour, Phil held a celebration party at which he threw a punch at a photographer from People magazine, who had deliberately jostled Phil's wife.

"I just went beserk! It was the end-of-tour crack-up, but I've never cracked in such an extreme manner before.

"Maybe I should do it more often though. One of the things I don't like about myself is that I do appear to be *too* nice! Maybe there should be more obvious nastiness in me. On the other hand, I don't really understand why it should be a dirty word for someone to say that I'm a nice bloke or a decent chap.

"There are certain things that are normal to me – on the last English tour that Genesis did, there were kids outside every night, waiting for two hours just to get our autographs. They probably got out of school or skived off work or whatever and they're waiting – you get out of a car and you have two choices: you either walk straight through

like people do and they would probably think 'Oh, he's a star, of course he's going to walk through' – or, you can stop and actually sign autographs and be a decent bloke, which is what I prefer to do.

"I'm always amazed by people saying 'I don't believe you stopped. You stopped! Ritchie Blackmore just pushed us out of the way.'

"We were playing this gig in Glasgow and there was a snooker championship going on. I love watching snooker on television. I'm not a snooker fan, but Alex Higgins fascinates me.

"Steve Davis was there and I said to him 'Can I have your autograph?' – and he didn't even look at me! To be fair, he was just about to have a match, but then I was just about to go on stage, so he said 'Have you got a pen?' and I hadn't, so I went and got one and he hadn't looked at me at this point. I didn't feel like saying 'Hey! I'm Phil Collins from Genesis, maybe you've heard of me', so I was just trying to get an autograph like a punter. He signed and still didn't look at me . . . so my impression of him now, whenever I see him on television, I'll always think of *that*.

"OK, we all have our down moments – one night outside Hammersmith Odeon, there were thirty or forty kids and I could have avoided them around the front, but my car was round the back – so I could either run for it and run them over or I could stop. And I'd been up in the bar drinking with everybody while they'd been out in the cold for an hour and a half – all you've got to do is take fifteen minutes and they all go home saying 'He wasn't a schmuck!'

"And that's what it boils down to, I don't want to be thought of as a schmuck. I want them to go away with a good memory of me, because that's the only time they're going to meet me: they can either leave with a nice feeling or a nasty feeling.

"And life just seems so much easier for everybody if they can leave with a nice feeling. So, to me, that's the normal way of doing things, that's not a surprising way. It's just being a normal person."

No-one would doubt Phil Collins is a normal person,

but he's also a hopeless – and hopeful – romantic.

"I'm very easily emotionally moved – even a film like 'The Alamo' with John Wayne brings tears to my eyes. And obviously a really big thing was when I got divorced. I don't believe it's wrong to cry. I don't think boys crying is anything to be ashamed of and I don't necessarily believe it's wrong to tell people you're unhappy; it's bad to bottle things up."

How would you like to be remembered?

"As a fair, honest bloke. That's it. I'm always shocked when someone kicks me in the teeth, because I'm not cynical – I have moments of cynicism, but most of the time I will be open, assuming that the other person will respond in the same way."

So – after everything else – who or what is Phil Collins? Drummer, clown, actor, singer, producer, international superstar, all-round entertainer?

"I'm a drummer," he replies without even pausing. "I'm better at that than anything else.

"With early Genesis, I wanted to show everybody I could play. Cobham and all that was happening, and I wanted to show that I could bat myself around the kit like he did. Although I never did it anywhere as well as he does.

"And when I listen back to Genesis, I find that there are songs where I should have laid back a little more than I actually wound up doing, just because I wanted to impress people. But I don't practise the drums at all. The only way to play the drums is to actually do it. To be a good drummer, you need natural intuition. It's really a case of primal instinct.

"Taking that to its logical conclusion, you come to things like 'In The Air Tonight', where I'm happy not to have any drums on it until the right moment. More often than not nowadays, I'm interested in the *sound* of the drums. I find if I've got a sound, I can make that thing musical.

"I think everybody has their capabilities, it's just a question of getting to know them. I know mine now and use them to their fullest extent.

"Second is writing, I think. It doesn't come easily to me,

but if you're asking me to analyse, I suppose I'm capable on occasions of saying things which strike a chord with people. I hope I write songs which tell stories. I like to try and write songs which sound like conversations.

"On *Face Value*, for example, a lot of people who had gone through a similar situation with their marriage breaking up said to me 'I've often felt that too, but I've never heard it put so conversationally'.

"I'm proud of that aspect of what I do. I'm not a great songwriter, full stop. But I sometimes put my finger on little buttons which hit nerves.

"Third is my singing, I enjoy being out front, singing my own songs, especially after years of being hidden behind a drum-kit! I was thrown in at the deep end a bit because I've played drums for twenty-five years but I only started singing in 1975. In the early days with Genesis, when I started singing, I was a very rhythmic, percussive singer – and I still am, though I'm getting better as a singer all the time. I sort of grew up to be a professional drummer and suddenly I'm a singer!

"There's things with my voice that I'm still overdoing but I am getting better though. I don't ever practise, though . . . I live in fear of a dodgy throat – we're onstage a long time, and it's mostly singing. I wrote the songs too, so I should be able to sing them!

"Singers are supposed to be a certain type of person – they're supposed to be the ones that move on stage. I mean, I just stand there and sing!

"They're the ones that the birds are supposed to fancy, but I never realy wanted to be part of that – you know, wiggling your bottom! Someone like Simon le Bon is sexually attractive to women, but I know what my limitations are. I know where I stand.

"I suppose the production duties rank about equal with singing. I actually don't find it that complicated a business. There's always been such an aura around producers – people like George Martin or Phil Spector.

"I tend to work more on instinct. We've all got a pair of ears, so it's really just a case of 'Does that sound right?', and 'What does this need to have added in there?' and so

on. My solo thing is the main thing, because it started on such a personal level; it's the thing that's most important to me. It's my personal expression, so it's bound to be dominant.

"But, equally, Genesis is more important to me than the production of someone else's record, because a third of the group is me."

"I could put on a persona that is moody and dark – but that isn't me! So what I'm saying is that the 'professional Londoner' actually *is* me – it's not because my theatrical training has taught me to play the part of a jolly cheeky chappie.

"As for acting – well, I've been sent film scripts, but I don't have the time to read them. And I don't want to do any of those Ringo parts or Roger Daltrey parts either. If I ever did a part, then I'd love to do something like Dudley Moore. Perhaps a romantic comedy . . . I think I'd be good at that sort of thing.

"As a matter of fact, I would like to have played the Jack Nicholson part in 'Terms Of Endearment' – he's one of my favourite actors."

Eventually, Phil not only found time to read a script, but discovered a script that he liked! It's not for a feature film, though, but for a part in the hit TV adventure series 'Miami Vice'.

I'm playing a game show host," explains Phil. "I'm not sure how good I'll be because I haven't acted for so long, but I've picked up some tips from comedian Steve Martin who reckons that to be a convincing game show host you have to laugh after every sentence.

"So I'll be saying lines like 'Well, it's great to be here tonight, ha-ha-ha!' and 'You're a terrific audience, haw-haw!'."

Following his success with 'Against All Odds', Phil's film connection was further strengthened by his musical contribution to the soundtrack of 'White Night', "a thriller with dance", starring Gregory Hines. Among other international artists such as Robert Plant, John Hiatt, Roberta Flack, Chaka Khan and Lou Reed, Phil contributed an emotional duet with Marilyn Martin called 'Separate

Lives' – which was subsequently released as a single.

Even allowing for natural modesty, Phil Collins claims that he is neither a great singer nor gifted songwriter – and yet he's one of the most-successful and best-loved modern pop performers in the world!

"I think people like me and I've been able to build up a following because I'm straight about what I do," he offers by way of explanation. "I'm determined, but I'm enthusiastic and honest.

"I think people can see I'm being honest. You know where you stand with me. The fact that I don't stop working endears me to people. I guess I'm a bit of a workaholic, at least that's often what I've been labelled. It's tiring and it's hard work . . . but it's not a hard life.

"I can't think of myself as a sex symbol; maybe the attraction is that I'm accessible and I'm a bit cuddly as well, or perhaps it's an affinity with the things that I write about. More likely it's sympathy – 'Aw poor Phil, look at his little face . . .'!

Do you hope you die before you get old?

"No. I don't hope that – I don't see that there's any reason for that. I'm sure that I'll be happy doing whatever I'm doing whenever I'm officially called old."

Is there any one thing that you haven't achieved yet that you still want?

"There has to be – how shallow a person I'd be if I said 'No, no, I've achieved everything in life . . .'."

But is Phil Collins a happy man?

"Oh yeah, happier . . . that situation five years ago when I went through my divorce, in some respects I'm loath to talk about it because people say I'm whingeing on, but I write songs as a result of what happened to me. That's why I write happy songs now."

15

MUSIC AROUND THE WORLD

For Phil Collins, what is there left to achieve?

Despite his own modest protests, he's done everything he could ever have dreamed of or wished for – and more. Number One hit singles, hit albums, sell-out world tours . . . all these both as a solo artist and as a member of Genesis. In 1985, he became the fifteenth UK artist to register simultaneous Number One positions in both the singles and albums charts in America, with 'Take Me Home' and *No Jacket Required*.

But recently Phil Collins made rock history and achieved something that no-one else has ever done: he appeared live on world-wide television twice in the one day in two different continents, and all for the benefit of starving millions in Africa. The marvellous Live Aid shows were the brainchild of Bob Geldof, but Phil Collins was their star, their crowning glory – positive proof that nice guys can be winners and that rock artists do still have a social conscience.

He'd already been actively involved in the million-selling Band Aid single 'Do They Know It's Christmas', on which he played drums – although he didn't sing on it at all.

"I'd just recorded duets with Philip Bailey and Eric Clapton and the record company were nagging me not to sing anything more until my own album came out, they were terrified I'd over-expose my voice. So I had to tell

Geldof 'Sorry Bob, I can't sing.'."

But when it came to 13th July 1985 – probably the greatest day in the history of pop music – Phil Collins was asked to do the impossible. Geldof wanted the two major shows in London and Philadelphia to have some kind of unity and continuity. He needed someone to play both shows in one day, and Phil was the only person with the immense popularity and the relaxed disposition to be able to deal with such a responsibility.

Appearing at Wembley Stadium in London in mid-afternoon, he sat at the piano, totally alone, and played 'In The Air Tonight' without any accompaniment at all, followed by 'Long Long Way To Go' on which he was joined by Sting on guitar and backing vocals. Phil then returned the compliment by singing on Sting's 'Every Breathe You Take' before dashing out of the stadium on his way to America – flying straight from London to New York by Concorde and swifly transferring to Philadelphia to play alongside such stars as Eric Clapton, Led Zeppelin and Madonna.

"After singing at Wembley, I arrived at Philadelphia at 7pm, got to the gig at ten past and Eric was on at 7.30! So I rushed to find out what he was playing and say 'ello. Then I rushed over to Robert Plant's caravan to see what Led Zeppelin were doing."

Phil Collins then ran on stage and proved why he's an international superstar loved by young and old. "I did it because I was asked to," he said. "That's why."

And all over the world, a million voices were raised in song:

'I can feel it coming in the air tonight, oh Lord . . .'

DISCOGRAPHY

GENESIS:

Albums:

Title	Label	Catalogue No	Release Date
1. **From Genesis To Revelation**	Decca	SKL 4990	March 1969
2. **Trespass**	Charisma	CAS 1020	October 1970
3. **Nursery Cryme**	Charisma	CAS 1052	November 1971
4. **Foxtrot**	Charisma	CAS 1058	October 1972
5. **Genesis Live**	Charisma	CLASS 1	August 1973
6. **Selling England By The Pound**	Charisma	CAS 1074	October 1973
7. **The Lamb Lies Down On Broadway**	Charisma	CGS 101	November 1974
8. **A Trick Of The Tail**	Charisma	CDS 4001	February 1976
9. **Wind And Wuthering**	Charisma	CDS 4005	December 1976
10. **Seconds Out**	Charisma	GE 2001	October 1977
11. **And Then There Were Three**	Charisma	CDS 4010	April 1978
12. **Duke**	Charisma	CBR 101	March 1980
13. **ABACAB**	Charisma	CBR 102	September 1981
14. **Three Sides Live**	Charisma	GE 1002	June 1982
15. **Genesis**	Charisma	GENLP 1	October 1983

Singles:

Title	Label	Catalogue No	Release Date
1. **The Silent Sun/** That's Me	Decca	F12735	22 February 1968
2. **A Winter's Tale/** One Eyed Hound	Decca	F12775	10 May 1969

Title	Label	Catalogue No	Release Date
3. **Where The Sour Turns To Sweet**/In Hiding	Decca	F12949	27 June 1969
4. **The Knife (Part I)**/The Knife (Part II)	Charisma	CB 152	1971
5. **I Know What I Like**/Twilight Alehouse	Charisma	CB 224	February 1974
6. **Counting Out Time**/Riding The Scree	Charisma	CB 238	November 1974
7. **The Carpet Crawlers**/Evil Jam (The Waiting Room live)	Charisma	CB 251	April 1975
8. **A Trick Of The Tail**/Ripples	Charisma	CB 277	March 1976
9. **Your Own Special Way**/It's Yourself	Charisma	CB 300	February 1977
10. **Spot The Pigeon** EP (Match Of The Day/Pigeons/Inside And Out	Charisma	GEN 001	May 1977
11. **Follow You Follow Me**/Ballad Of Big	Charisma	CB 309	March 1978
12. **Many Too Many**/The Day Light Went Out/Vancouver	Charisma	CB 315	June 1978
13. **Turn It On Again**/Behind The Lines (Part II)	Charisma	CB 356	March 1980
14. **Duchess**/Open Door	Charisma	CB 363	May 1980
15. **Misunderstanding**/Evidence Of Autumn	Charisma	CB 369	August 1980
16. **ABACAB**/Another Record	Charisma	CB 388	August 1981
17. **Keep It Dark**/Naminanu	Charisma	CB 391	October 1981
18. **Man On The Corner**/Submarine	Charisma	CB 393	March 1982
19. **3 × 3** EP (Paperlate/You Might Recall/Me And Virgil)	Charisma	GEN1	May 1982
20. **Mama**/It's Gonna Get Better	Charisma/Virgin	MAMA1	August 1983
21. **That's All**/Taking It All Too Hard	Charisma/Virgin	TATA1	November 1983
22. **Illegal Alien**/Turn It On Again (live)	Charisma/Virgin	AL1	January 1984

FLAMING YOUTH:

Album:

Title	Label	Catalogue No	Release Date
Ark II	Fontana	STL 5533	November 1969

Single:

Title	Label	Catalogue No	Release Date
Guide Me Orion	Fontana	TF 1057	November 1969

BRAND X:

Albums:

Title	Label	Catalogue No	Release Date
1. Unorthodox Behaviour	Charisma	CAS 1117	July 1976
2. Moroccan Roll	Charisma	CAS 1126	April 1977
3. Livestock	Charisma	CLASS 5	November 1977
4. Masques (NB: Phil Collins does not appear on this Brand X album.)	Charisma	CAS 1138	September 1978
5. Product	Charisma	CAS 1147	September 1979
6. Do They Hurt?	Charisma	CAS 1151	May 1980
7. Is There Anything About?	CBS	CBS 85967	September 1982

Single:

Title	Label	Catalogue No	Release Date
Soho/ Dance Of The Illegal Aliens	Charisma	CB 340	September 1979

PHIL COLLINS AS A SOLO ARTIST:

Albums:

Title	Label	Catalogue No	Release Date
1. Face Value	Virgin	V2185	February 1981
2. Hello, I Must Be Going	Virgin	V2252	November 1982
3. No Jacket Required	Virgin	V2345	April 1985

Singles:

Title	Label	Catalogue No	Release Date
1. In The Air Tonight/ The Roof Is Leaking	Virgin	VSK 102	January 1981
2. I Missed Again/ I'm Not Moving	Virgin	VS 402	March 1981
3. If Leaving Me Is Easy/ Drawingboard	Virgin	VS 423	May 1981
4. Thru' These Walls/ Do You Know, Do You Care?	Virgin	VS 524	October 1982
5. You Can't Hurry Love/ I Cannot Believe It's True	Virgin	VS 531	November 1982
6. Don't Let Him Steal Your Heart Away/Thunder And Lightning	Virgin	VS 572	March 1983
7. Why Can't It Wait 'Til Morning?/Like China	Virgin	VS 603	May 1983
8. Against All Odds/ Making A Big Mistake	Virgin	VS 674	March 1984
9. Sussudio/ The Man With The Horn	Virgin	VS 736	January 1985
10. Easy Lover/ Woman (duet with Philip Bailey)	CBS	A&TA 4915	February 1985
11. One More Night/ I Like The Way	Virgin	VS 755	April 1985
12. Take Me Home/ He Said Hello Goodbye	Virgin	VS 777	July 1985

For further details of production duties and session work by not only Phil Collins but all the other members (and ex-members) of Genesis, readers are recommended to consult 'Turn It On Again' by Geoff Parkyn.

Titles, release dates and catalogue numbers relate to UK releases only – details vary in other parts of the world.